M000014269

<u>20 Jobs: A Memoir</u>

G. H. Ashenfelter

Copyright © Text G.H. Ashenfelter 2017

Copyright © Photographs G.H. Ashenfelter 2017

The author asserts the moral right under the Copyright, Designs and Patents Act 1988 to be identified as the author of this work.

All rights reserved. No part of this publication may be reproduced, stored in a retrieval system, or transmitted, in any form or by any means without the prior written consent of the author, nor be otherwise circulated in any form of binding or cover other than that in which it is published and without a similar condition being imposed on the subsequent purchaser.

Acknowledgments

Without my family and friends in my life, I could never have written this story. They are my inspiration.

Also, I'm so grateful for the members of the Family Folklore group at the Stow-Munroe Falls Public Library. They listened patiently to every draft and encouraged me to keep writing. I would not have succeeded in writing and finishing this book without their support.

A special thanks for the extensive line editing from Tina Lucas and for other editing help from Jenny, Joyce and Kathy. I am blessed with terrific friends.

For my dad

And my children and grandchildren
Share your stories – they are your life

CONTENTS

Beginnings   2

Job 1 – Carhop   12
Job 2 – Riviera Cabana Club   23
Job 3 – Kresge's   30
Job 4 – The Stencil Factory   41
Job 5 - Kresge's #2   48
Job 6 – Kenny Kings   55
Job 7 – Howard Johnson's   60
Job 8 – Northfield Race Track   71
Job 9 – Celery Picker   85
Job 10 – Howard Johnson's Turnpike   95
Job 11 – Western Reserve Electronics   103
Job 12 – General Electric – Part 1   117
Job 13 – Lindy's Bar   129
Job 12 - General Electric Continued – Part 2   139
Job 14 – Trailer Park Office Assistant   153
Job 15 – Cuyahoga Falls High School   159
Job 16 – Sylvan Learning Center   180
Job 17 – Camp Asbury   190
Job 18 - Summer School   205
Job 19 – GED Class   221
Job 20 – Electronic Classroom of Tomorrow   231

"The World is moved along, not only by the mighty shove of its heroes, but also by the aggregate of tiny pushes of each honest worker."

~ Helen Keller

"The next thing most like living one's life over again seems to be a recollection of that life, and to make that recollection as durable as possible by putting it down in writing."

~ Ben Franklin

G.H. Ashenfelter

Memories . . .
Soothe like sweet tea
On a hot summer's day.
Feel bitter like sin
When you kneel down to pray.

Memories . . .
Stand by your side
When you wish them away,
And crouch down low
When you bid them to stay.

Memories . . .
Stab at your chest
On the happiest day,
But can heal you the best.
Don't throw them away.

Beginnings

Life can be recorded and remembered in many ways. One way would be to step on the time chart and chronicle your life year by year. Another way would be to waltz through life in the arms of your lovers, beat by beat. You can also recount a life by remembering each triumph and defeat. None of these would work well for my life story. For me, looking back, life can only be divided up job by job. My life had no exceptional triumphs and no special love stories. True, there were men who loved me well enough, but not with the kind of love that inspires great literature or riveting memoirs. Consequently, for this memoir, my life will be measured out by paydays and workdays and dishes in the sink. You may wonder how I decided on this unusual organizational pattern.

It started one afternoon as I sat next to my dad at a neighborhood Greek-style restaurant, the Acropolis. A large mural of fake Grecian vineyards and purple grapes created our backdrop. Waiting for our lunch to arrive, I fidgeted with the paper place mats and straightened up the fork and knife next to the napkin. I had run out of conversation. I looked over and observed my dad. He was a nice looking man of 70 with wavy brown hair and a thin tan face that slightly resembled Pope Paul. He looked totally Polish, which he was. Dad sat straight in his chair and didn't look like a dowdy senior citizen; he still walked with vigor and never slouched from his six foot height. Since his second wife, Ruth, passed away after a long struggle with her health, he seemed more relaxed. This was a man who had worked hard all his life. After he divorced his first wife, Almanda, my mom, he then remarried and was on the verge of divorcing his second wife until she became seriously ill. Because of her illness, he stayed with her and supported her until she passed away.

Dad had fought major health battles with cancer and was a survivor. Now retired, he spent his time, like many seniors, puttering around the garden, feeding the birds and the stray cats. He especially liked visiting his children, playing euchre and trying to win money by opening tickets at the Moose Club. He lived a peaceful life in his little mobile home park and had a new love life complete with a special friend, otherwise, a girlfriend. He seemed happy. I, on the other hand, was not happy with my life at this time. I was slowly recovering from a broken marriage and had no special friend.

As the silence continued, it seemed a choice time for a father-daughter talk. I turned my chair to face Dad, cleared my throat and decided to ask one of those questions that men usually don't like to answer. For the first time in my life, I casually said, "So, Dad, tell me about your life." I waited with a little smile of anticipation. I was ready to hear all about the romance and our intimate family details, how he met my mom and how excited he was when we, his precious children, arrived.

With nothing else to talk about at this time, Dad seemed to like this spotlight opportunity to tell his story. He started by telling me about his jobs throughout his lifetime and ended with the same subject. No glamour, no love, and no mention of "you were born on a lovely spring day." Nope, it was all about his jobs, all three of them.

Dad's life story began at age 14. In 1931 he lost his father Julius to tuberculosis or TB, which is an infectious lung disease that is currently controlled in our modern world thanks to antibiotics. After his father's death, my dad quit school, left his stepmother and went to seek his fortune in the nearby dairy farms of upstate New York. He talked about the places he worked, first at a cheese factory in Lowville and then on one farm or another. This was in the early '30s. Dad didn't give details about how it was to work in cow barns, but he didn't need to. I had experienced the milking routine from my childhood visits to my maternal grandmother's farm in New York - the same farm where my dad worked when he met my mom.

At a young age, I learned the routine from my uncles as they milked the cows. My main chore was to lug the shiny buckets sloshing over with milk as I stepped carefully around cow pies buzzing with flies. My eyes widened with amazement when the cows opened their sphincters and often overshot the manure gutter making the cement floor slippery and smelly like a jungle path after rain. Dad didn't need to elaborate on the milking routine for me. I remembered pouring the milk through filters into giant metal cans to strain out the bits of straw and dead flies. The giant milk cans were then hoisted into a huge cold spring water cooler to preserve the warm, frothy white lifeblood of the dairy farmer. Even today, I can smell the sweet fresh hay and the heady aroma of manure mixed in with the soft sounds of cows mooing their crooning song. It was exotic to a child. He didn't have to include these details because I lived them while visiting my grandmother's farm as a child.

What I really wanted to hear was more about the family and how Dad met my mom. I knew he worked at her family's dairy farm on Tug Hill. Once, my Aunt Vera told me that he named all the new calves Almanda, after my mom. Dad didn't mention that part or even tell how they met. At one point my mom entered the story line and I found out they ran away to get married without telling her parents. This was new family information and kind of romantic. Would her parents have disapproved of my hard-working dad? Probably not, because Dad said that when they found out about the marriage her parents threw them a wedding shindig.

I remembered looking at an old black and white photo. Mom was standing in the middle between a young version of my dad and her father, Ladette. She had her arms folded tight across her chest. Dad and Grandpa both leaned in close to mom with their drinks raised high in celebration. Dad had his arm around Mom's shoulder holding her tight. He looked dashing in a high collar white shirt, dark trousers and a dark tie. His hair appeared freshly cut and parted over to one side. Mom wore a long white skirt and high necked blouse with a fancy, flared out bow-like collar. Her hair was parted down the middle and pulled back in a bun. Her father was decked out in a white shirt, black tie and dark pants. The picture was not marked in any way, so I'm not sure if it was their wedding celebration, but in my mind, it is. Henry and Almanda joined together as man and wife - my mom and dad.

Dad's story did not include any details about the wedding celebration. Instead, his story line turned back to his work. He found a job working for an Italian guy who owned a construction company. Dad liked his boss and his new job as an apprentice mechanic repairing heavy duty construction equipment. His employment took place during the time of the Great Depression, because Dad repeatedly told me how lucky he was to be working when so many men were out of work. In 1933, when the Great Depression reached its peak, some 13 to 15 million Americans were unemployed and nearly half of the country's banks had failed.

Dad told me that his Italian boss had to sell the company and the new owner moved the company out of state. So in order to keep his job, Dad and Mom moved with the company. I never thought about it before, but this must be how we ended up in Ohio. Did my mom hate leaving the farm, her parents, her five brothers and only sister? Did she feel alienated or afraid moving from the country into a town? She never mentioned it if she did. Mom did not tell many family stories, at least not to me. During this conversation with Dad, some of our family history was coming to light even though the story wasn't about me as I had hoped.

Not really a storyteller, Dad didn't embellish the facts or even mention when my older sister Betty and I were born. He and Mom moved on with the construction company and that was just how it was. More than once, Dad stressed how lucky he was to be working during the depression and the fact that we never had to go without. I could tell that this meant a lot to him. He had a decent job and they were hard to come by in those days. A job was important! When the construction company moved to Solon, Ohio, Dad and Mom followed along with the earth moving equipment to settle in Bedford, a suburb of Cleveland. They did this because it was Dad's job, his new profession, and a decent pay check.

Our lunch arrived and story time ended. I never asked Dad to tell me about his life again. He did tell me some family stories, but they were more about his younger days, before Mom. My mom died when she was only 50, a combination of heart failure, kidney failure, liver failure and divorce. Her main inheritance from her family on Tug Hill was the legacy of hard work, drinking and smoking. Would my parents' lives and mine been different if Dad had never followed along with the construction company? Could we have ended up living on Tug Hill like the relatives that I so loved to visit? Farmer kids driving tractors instead of townie kids riding bikes? Dad's choice of jobs shaped our family's future.

As we ate our meal, a picture of a white, two-story house on Magnolia Street in Bedford popped into my head with a little me sitting outside beside the driveway, writing on the sidewalk with stones, waiting for Dad's green Chevy panel truck, with Acme Construction Company painted in bold white letters on the side, to come gliding in. I jumped up as soon as I saw him. Tall, handsome and slender, my dad, wearing his one piece, brown work uniform and hat, unfolded from the driver's seat and grinned when he saw me. I ran to Dad for a hug, smelling the grease and sweat on his clothes. He gave me a quick embrace and headed for the basement shower where he scrubbed his hands with pumice and industrial strength Gojo Soap until the black grease disappeared from beneath his fingernails. He was now cleaned up for our evening meal.

Mom had supper on the table, all home cooked; we were, after all, the typical family of the '50s. She stayed home to make meals, do laundry and keep up the house while Dad worked at his construction job and kept up the lawn. My mom had her own job at home. We had six bedrooms in our house and she took in boarders, men who worked at the Walton Hills Ford Plant. They rented our spare rooms, which gave Mom plenty to do: cooking, cleaning and keeping up with piles of laundry washed in a wringer washer and hung out on a line to dry. She wore flowered print dresses covered up with an apron over her full figure. Her medium length, brown hair was pulled up with combs on the sides. She smelled like Jergens Lotion, a flowery scent I still love today; and Camel cigarettes, a strong odor that made me push mom away. As a kid my job was to get outside and play and stay out from under her feet. Mom never taught me to cook or bake, but maybe I never expressed an interest in learning household skills. I'm not sure which.

Mom and dad had four children that survived. First, my sister Betty was born in 1939 and then four years later me, or Little Gladys, as I was called since I was named after my Aunt Gladys. A few years after I was born, Mom lost an infant son and later, a set of twin boys. I try to imagine having four brothers instead of one. That would have changed our family dynamics for sure. Finally, nine years after I was born, my brother Joe arrived in our family and everyone was overjoyed, except for me.

My youngest kid status was wiped off the slate with the arrival of a much-desired boy. Betty was thrilled about having a baby brother and insisted we call him Joe, his middle name, instead of his given name, Henry, after my dad. At Betty's insistence, the name Joe stuck. Like Betty, Joe ended up getting his own way, but instead of being strong-willed, he was spoiled by Betty and Dad. They gave in to his every demand.

Two years after Joe was born, my little sister Jane came along, a pretty little blonde. I'd like to say that since she was the youngest and the only one of us with blonde hair, that she was spoiled like Joe. That didn't happen though. The spotlight remained on Joe, the only boy. Unfortunately, Joe made Jane's younger life a misery as he teased her constantly and nobody stopped him. Why? Probably because Mom and Dad were going through a divorce and discipline was not the same as when I was younger. Joe and Jane missed out on our earlier family life when Mom was our main disciplinarian. I can remember running up our steps, two at a time, lickety-bang with my mom close on my heels and the belt whipping around my legs. We behaved or we got the belt. Dad was more lenient.

Before Joe and Jane came along, I thought that I was Dad's favorite. My best memory was when he took me with him to his work at Acme Construction Company. I was so excited. Inside the cavernous shop, I fingered the shiny, greasy nuts and bolts sitting in the assorted bins. Everything I touched was oily and the metal smelled so strong I could taste it on my tongue. This was how Dad smelled, like grease and metal. I liked the smell. Dad warned me not to mix up the parts and I was very careful not to do that. Visiting Dad's work became more entertaining when I discovered the creeper. It was like a little wooden sled on wheels that sat about four inches off the floor. Men could lie on their backs and slide under the equipment to do repairs. I sat on it and scooted around the shop in a crazy, zigzag fashion. Dad quickly put a stop to that nonsense.

Little did I know, years down the road that little creeper would cause the end of my dad's work career when he stepped on it, fell backwards and broke a bone in his thigh. That injury forced him to retire from his third and last job at Acme Construction Company.

Looking back at my life as Dad had done, I realize my jobs influenced my life choices and therefore my destiny. During my 18 years of marriage, I raised four children and stayed home to do housework, which in spite of the name "work" does not count for gainful employment on a Social Security statement. Housewife or motherhood is not counted in my list of jobs even though they were the most challenging professions I tackled. Before, during and after being a housewife and mother, I worked at twenty separate jobs.

I find it easier to view my life as it evolved job by job. I am my father's daughter after all. For me, this is the best, or perhaps the only way I can write my life story, starting with my first job as a teen and ending with my last job before retirement. Join me now on this lifetime journey, job by job and chapter by chapter.

20 Jobs: A Memoir

Job 1 – Carhop

It's summer, 1957, I'm out of school and ready to do what I always did, sleep late, eat butterscotch sundaes at the Glendale Sweet Shop, listen to the jukebox play "Blue Suede Shoes" or "16 Tons" and read and read some more. I devoured all the comic books I could get my sticky hands on. Comics like Casper, Superman and especially Archie. One character in the Archie comic book, Veronica, was my favorite with her long dark hair, shapely body and brains. Why would the guys even consider Betty, the curvy blonde, over Veronica? I'm 14, not blonde, not shapely, but happy to be me.

My current niche was 9th grade in high school where I made the honor roll, mainly because I enjoyed studying and reading. My best subject was Latin, and I spent hours laying across my bed memorizing vocabulary and rolling the amo, amos, amat verbs around on my tongue. I even went outside my comfort zone and adorned a blue sheet as a toga for the 9th grade Latin Club party. Life was easy and sweet for a 14-year-old as the summer rolled in. Little did I know that my older sister, Betty, had a different plan for my summer of '57, a job.

Betty and I were not close as sisters go; in fact we fought most of our lives. It started very early when my mom proudly wrote in my baby book that Uncle Stanley and Aunt Gladys gave me a US Savings Bond and a dress, and that my older sister Betty gave me a black eye, like it was another present. Welcome to the family, baby girl, and watch out for your big sister. It was not easy to follow along on Betty's heels and be her little sister. For survival, I learned to stay out of her way as much as possible. She was a strong-willed, tough and independent teen with hobbies like fast cars, horses and boys. She commanded them all to do what she wanted.

Unlike me, Betty hated reading and quit high school at age16. She then convinced Mom and Dad to let her get a job and a car. Now at 18, she drove a sharp, cool looking, white '56 Chevy convertible with a continental kit, glass pack muffler and fender skirts along with the chrome V stripe down the side. Most of the time if it wasn't raining, she had the top down so she was more visible. I can picture Betty's long, straight, black hair flying in the wind like an Indian princess as she drag raced her car down Broadway or flew across the meadow on her horse Midnight. Sometimes she allowed me to ride with her, but I always had to sit in the back seat where the wind whipped my hair in every direction. I ducked down on the floor to keep warm and stay out of sight.

A legend in our little town, Betty had speeding tickets issued by the Walton Hills Police proudly taped all over the walls of her bedroom. The cops knew her on a first name basis. On the other hand, I was her nondescript, studious, mousy little sister and that status was fine with me.

Betty worked as a waitress at Ginny's in Northfield, the hangout drive-in restaurant for teens in our area. Ginny's burgers were the first cousins of the Big Boy, Whopper and Big Mac. The main difference between burgers now and then was that Ginny's burgers were made with real, fresh hamburger meat that tasted like heaven - all adorned with Ginny's secret sauce and shredded lettuce on a toasted sesame seed bun. It makes my mouth water to think how delicious they tasted. Add a side of crispy, real batter-dipped onion rings or fresh cut French fries, never frozen. Then top that off with red glazed, homemade fresh strawberry pie. Food for the gods! It was a popular drive-in restaurant in those days.

Ginny's had indoor and outdoor dining featuring carhop service where customers could eat burgers, fries and milkshakes directly from the metal tray attached to the window of the car. Younger, inexperienced girls started out first as car hops and then worked up to inside dining room server where there was jukebox music, no rain and bigger tips. Betty was the top waitress working inside at Ginny's and had lots of influence, enough to land her little sister a job. That was how I started work at age 14, not because I wanted to be a carhop or anything really, but because my sister thought I needed to stop sitting around reading so much and get off my lazy butt and work.

"Get up! You have to go to work today!" My sister Betty shouted up the steps for me to get out of bed for my first day of work at Ginny's. I pulled the covers over my head and tried to drown out her voice. Oh, No! I thought summer mornings were for sleeping, but I knew it was no use arguing with my hard-headed sister. I dragged myself out of the rumpled sheets and started to dress. First I put on and buttoned up my white blouse, freshly ironed from the night before. Then I squeezed into my black peg-leg pants with the little zippers up the ankle sides. Bobby socks and saddle shoes were next. Pulling my hair back in a pony tail, I was resigned to my fate. Okay, I'm ready, I groaned, as I slowly descended the stairs, not sure what was in store on my first day as a working girl.

Ginny's was not only the name of the restaurant, but the name of a real person. Luckily, she was there to help me on my first morning. Not knowing what to expect, I stood there, like a black and white picture in freeze frame. Ginny wore a large white apron over her dress. She had a strong face and dark, medium length hair pulled back in a hair net. She patiently explained the routine of taking orders from customers. I was shown how to write down the food order on a green, lined paper pad that was kept in my black, cloth pouch that fastened around my waist on a belt. On this belt, a shiny metal changer was attached with individual slots for nickels, dimes, quarters, and pennies. It was heavy with the weight of first responsibility. I pushed the little levers, and click, click, click, the change popped out of the slots at the bottom. It felt strange and bulky as it hung down from my waist.

"Any questions, sweetie?" Ginny tried to look directly in my eyes. I looked down towards the floor and mumbled that I understood. She was putting her trust in me and I didn't want to disappoint her or appear ignorant. In reality, I was somewhat lost about my duties. Tell me what to do and I'll just do it, I thought to myself.

At first, all I had to do was stand and look out the big window and watch for a car to drive in and flash its lights, the signal for service. There was a service counter separating our car hop area from the kitchen, a narrow aisle and two doors, one marked In and one marked Out to prevent collisions. On the other side of the service counter, the kitchen bustled; I stood still waiting for a car to appear. Ginny who was in constant motion sensed my nervous inactivity and called me over to the kitchen side to help clean strawberries. An easy enough task if I had ever worked with a paring knife to clean a strawberry or anything. I had not. My cooking background was limited to making toast.

Most days, mom sent me outside to get out of her way. I came back home at supper time to eat the already prepared meal. Remember, my mom was not the "teach-your-daughter to cook" type of person. If I was underfoot in the kitchen, she usually shooed me out. To be fair, I did have some chores and knew how to wash dishes and windows. I remember doing them both slowly and methodically one piece of silverware, one pane of glass at a time, rubbing them over and over until completely clean and shiny. This was my way of working, no hurry, no pressure and no paring knife. I didn't admit this to Ginny.

No, cleaning strawberries was easy and any idiot could do it, but for my hands, it presented a challenge. How do I hold a paring knife and why do these darn berries keep squishing up, staining my fingers. I looked like a kid who ate too many cherry popsicles without the paper holder. I was glad when a car finally arrived that needed my attention. Hastily I wiped off the juice and fled through the Out door to take my first order of the day. My hands shook a little as I fumbled with the pencil and the green order pad. The couple ordered the usual burgers, fries and Cokes. I wrote down each item along with what they wanted on their burgers, went back inside through the In door, tucked the green slip under the clothespin clip, and waited.

The order was filled quickly in Ginny's efficient kitchen and I delivered the first tray of food and it hooked easily on the window of the car. I collected the money, tucked it inside my black pouch, made change with my cool silver change machine and breathed a sigh of relief. All that was left after that was to watch that car for any flashing lights so I could run out, unhook the tray and collect my tip. My eyes were riveted to that car. I wasn't having fun, but work was not supposed to be fun, was it?

∞∞∞∞∞∞∞∞∞

When I was a kid, a good deal of my time was spent lying in the grass in the back yard watching colonies of ants. I was nose to nose with the insect world and fascinated by their constant movement between the blades of grass, dandelions and clover. They built sand castles outside their mysterious underground caverns and came in and out of the sandy gates like merchants and traders in search of exotic treasures. I peered down as they scavenged for food and tugged huge pieces of anonymous particles over treacherous terrain. Playing god, I would put an obstacle in their way like a rock, fat stick, or a giant hand; trying not to hurt them but sometimes getting too close and taking out a tiny body part. If I maimed the ant badly, I squished it to take it out of its squirmy pain. I didn't like to do that, but hey, sorry. I was, after all, god of their world. They took it in stride as they adjusted their course, limping on four legs instead of six, on through the jungle lawn, up and over the inconvenience. Their little ant lives consisted of hurry and work and the huge hand of fate, or god, did not stop that fact.

∞∞∞∞∞∞∞∞∞

G.H. Ashenfelter

My first afternoon as a carhop proceeded with a car here and a car there, keeping me busy, but not rushed. It was getting close to 5:00, the end of my shift, when the giant hand dropped on me. One by one, cars pulled into the parking lot and put on their lights for service. Oh, no! I have to get their orders right away. I quickly ran from '56 Chevy to '55 Ford to '53 Buick, greeting the faceless customers and taking order after order. My mind ignored the panic that was rising in my gut. When those orders were turned in, I raced around the parking lot waiting on even more cars and turning in even more orders. The counter was soon filled up with metal trays full of fragrant burgers and fries waiting to be delivered. Flushed with heat, I picked up the first tray to deliver it and suddenly couldn't remember which car had ordered what or where to take the food. Why didn't I write down that tiny bit of information on my little green, lined pad? Now that giant hand of fate was blocking my path and making me squirm.

In my numbness, I tried to fix my blunder and scurried around much like the ants, but it was all a blur. I don't remember exactly when the evening shift of carhops arrived, but they did. Capable, real carhops who were smart enough to write down license plate numbers or colors of cars. They were my saviors as they grabbed trays of food and ran around the parking lot asking each customer what they had ordered. They straightened out my mixed up orders, and I don't even remember if I thanked them. Most messes and work days do come to an end at some point and this first one did too.

20 Jobs: A Memoir

As I rode home sitting silently next to my mom, she asked about my day. I looked down at my lap with the paper cup full of tips between my knees and mumbled it was fine, not wanting to admit my failure as a carhop. We didn't share feelings in our family so I didn't expect any sympathy or encouragement. Better to keep quiet. Mom stopped asking and drove silently as she puffed on her Camel cigarette. Later that week, I spent my tips on comic books, penny candy and butterscotch sundaes, but on the ride home from my first day of work, the tips seemed worthless. I wasn't sure they were an even trade for my freedom.

After that first day, my lesson learned, I made it a point to write down the license plate number or color of car that I waited on. But sometimes cars were sneaky and moved to another spot causing the panic to rise in my throat again until I found them. But now I was in control of this job, semi-efficient and finally able to clean a strawberry without mutilating it beyond recognition. I settled into being a carhop and started to enjoy earning my own money.

Betty occasionally allowed me to ride to work with her in her cool '56 Chevy convertible and even let me drive, but only once. Her car was a stick shift and my left leg shook uncontrollably as I concentrated so hard on trying to let out the clutch that I forgot to steer and ran it straight into the curb. That was the end of my driving lessons. Even though she never let me drive her convertible again, I didn't care. It scared me to drive.

G.H. Ashenfelter

In the middle of my carhop summer I discovered boys and the power that they had over me. One evening after working at Ginny's, Betty and I stopped at Frankie's, a little store and restaurant in Northfield Village close to Ginny's. While we were in the store, a boy named Pat looked in my direction and an unknown feeling swept over me. The hormones, what I call it now, or magic arrows, what I called it then, hit me hard. Pat had intense eyes and slicked back hair like Elvis; my stomach did flip flops. The fact that his one front tooth was missing didn't even faze me. He looked super cool. I was smitten and had no idea why. How could one little look carry so much clout and cause such disturbing emotions? Pat talked to Betty, but he kept glancing in my direction. I met his gaze, blushed and quickly looked down at my feet. I stood there, speechless as usual.

Shortly after that brief encounter at Frankie's, Pat started coming over to our house. I was sure he was there to see Betty, as I couldn't imagine anyone would be interested in me. One afternoon Pat and I were alone on the front porch. I sat perched up on the wooden railing and he stood close beside me. I don't remember any conversation. I didn't know how to talk to boys. Suddenly, for whatever strange reason, Pat leaned over and kissed me. My reaction was not what I expected, and probably not what he expected either. I slapped him hard, jumped down, and ran into the house and up the stairs to my bedroom where

I plopped face down on my messy bed amid my comic books. My insides wobbled with a new-found passion. At that moment my childhood world changed from unreal comic book plots to first real kisses.

Summer came to a close and my teen infatuation with Pat did not turn out well. I found out that he liked another girl in Northfield much better than me. Looking back, I realize it was puppy love, but at the time my feelings and pain felt very real.

The only thing I knew for sure at the end of my 14th summer was that I could be an efficient carhop and earn cups full of nickels, dimes and quarters. In addition, I learned that I could attract boys. What I could not do was handle the emotions caused by boys and first kisses. They scared me like driving a stick shift car and running it into a curb.

Job 2 – Riviera Cabana Club

The next summer, I didn't return to my job as a carhop at Ginny's Drive In. My sister Betty worked at a new place, so in her kindness toward her little sister, she found new employment for me. I would rather have gone back to being a carhop, or better yet, stayed home. But in my 15th summer, thanks to Betty, I started working in the snack bar at the Riviera Cabana Club in Solon. I was not excited about giving up my summer vacation time again, but there I was, stuck behind the snack counter at a fancy swim club.

Riviera means a coastal region frequented as a resort area and marked by mild climate, like in Southern France. This is not exactly an accurate description of Ohio, a Midwestern state known by the adage: if you don't like the weather, stick around, it will change. Cabana is a Spanish word that means literally a hut or a shelter resembling a cabin with an open side facing a beach or swimming pool. At the

Riviera Cabana Club it meant painted lockers of every color: green, blue, orange, and pink, which surrounded a cement pool filled with crystal, clear blue water - an ostentatious setting, my new place of employment.

My first Sunday morning working at the Riviera Club behind the snack counter started off quietly. I polished up the countertops and gazed out over the empty, sun drenched pool. The water was blue and inviting, but not to me. I wished that I could be any place else but here. Then a dark haired, tanned man in a short-sleeved, white shirt and khaki shorts approached the snack bar with this strange request.

"I'd like an order of lox and bagels,"

What? What did he ask for? I wondered to myself. Is he speaking a foreign language?

"What, sir?" I asked out loud.

"Lox and bagels," he repeated.

I asked him to repeat the request at least three more times and still didn't understand. What was he talking about? I had heard the word "locks," but never in connection with food, only on doors. The term "bagel" was not in my vocabulary at all. I could tell he was irritated as he looked at me like I was from another planet.

"Just a minute, sir," I finally muttered and went to find help from my sister who was in the back room. "Betty, what in the heck are locks and bagels?" She shook her head and shot me the "oh, you are so dumb" look. Then she brought out some

24

round, brown donut looking things along with a pink layer of raw looking fish.

"Oh, Yuck!" I said. "Do people really eat this stuff for breakfast?"

It turned out that they did, I realized, as Betty showed me how to toast the bagel, top it with the shiny, raw fish and garnish the strange concoction with a side of cream cheese. The man drummed his fingers impatiently on the counter top as he watched us. I turned and served it to him and mumbled my apologies. These new food items, lox and bagels, began my education of Jewish food; however, my grasp of Jewish cultural differences remained null and void. I learned how to toast the foreign bagels and top them with thin pink salmon served with a side of cream cheese, but never once ate them.

Most of the members of the Riviera Cabana Club were Jewish, and what I knew about Jewish people was . . . well nothing really. As for World War II, all I knew about that war was what I had seen in news reels that ran at the Stillwell Movie Theater in Bedford. Before each movie, I hunkered down in my seat in the dark theater and watched the world news that previewed each main movie. My only former view of the world outside of Bedford were these black and white images: noisy tanks, soldiers marching in matching uniforms with rifles and helmets, foreign places billowing with smoke and fire coming from ruined buildings, a bomb that created a big mushroom cloud. They were frightening scenes, but had nothing to do with me, I reasoned. Nobody explained to me what war was about or told me the horrific fact that approximately six million Jews were killed in WWII. My isolated world was safe and sane and it didn't include the term Holocaust. I had no idea what it meant to be Jewish!

To me, at the time, these Bermuda shorts clad people seemed aloof and snobby. They barely talked to me except to order food. To be fair, I was not an outgoing person, merely a shy teen with limited knowledge of different cultures. Organized, traditional religion was not part of my upbringing since my family didn't attend church. My dad was raised Catholic, but he married Mom outside the Catholic Church, so according to the Catholic doctrine, they were not even married.

A few times I attended a Catholic mass with my dad's brother, Uncle Stanley, and his wife, Aunt Gladys, my namesake. With no background or education in Catholicism, the service was meaningless, especially since it was spoken in Latin at the time. The ornate church and pungent incense smells made me feel strange and dizzy. Women always kept their heads covered with a hat or scarf, so Aunt Gladys would lend me a scarf or hankie to cover my hair. How silly that seemed to me. Why would women need to cover their hair?

My aunt and uncle paused at the end of the pew to genuflect, another mystery. I tried unsuccessfully to copy their movements by quickly moving my hand in a circle from my forehead to my shoulders and chest. I was not familiar with the

Father, Son and Holy Ghost concept. What was that all about, I wondered? All of that, along with the Latin words and the ceremonial service were peculiar to me, like the atmosphere of the club where I now worked.

The Riviera Cabana Club members were part of a world where I didn't belong - or understand. Our family never went to an exclusive pool or club. When we were younger, Betty and I swam at a sandy-bottomed outdoor lake, Lake Plada, where my mom casually dropped us off and left me in the care of my older sister who constantly tried to drown me. Betty amused herself by pushing my head under water or pulling me around by my pony tail. I became skilled at hiding from her among the swimmers and quickly learned to swim, at least dog paddle, for survival. Lake Plada was filled with noisy, splashing kids and the warm, grassy smells of summer. Often I lay for hours on the blanket, daydreaming and staring up at the myriad shapes of clouds drifting across the blue skies, feeling the sun beat down on my skin.

Lake Plada was the total opposite of the Riviera Cabana Club's concrete landscape with its sterile pool, brightly colored lockers and peculiar people dressed in stylish summer outfits and expensive bathing suits. They lounged on chairs adorned with color-splashed beach towels and never acknowledged that I existed until they needed a sandwich or soda to drink.

After Ginny's Drive In, time at the Cabana Club was slow paced, sun drenched and drop-dead boring. I missed the camaraderie of the carhop world and the hustle and bustle of Ginny's. My sister Betty often described her time working the Cabana Club as a "blast" since her best friend Carol worked with her. They were flirting, swimming, and enjoying themselves immensely. They were the managers and I was the peon behind the snack bar counter who longed for quitting time to escape and go home to read my books or sleep.

The summers no longer belonged to me and I mourned my loss of freedom and childhood. The jukebox was the only thing that brought me some solace. When it was cloudy, cool, or drizzly outside, business was slow. When the teens didn't need chips or pop, and the adults were not in the mood for lox and bagels, I would play slow songs on the juke box like Julie London's "Cry Me a River" or "The Man That Got Away." Over and over as I wiped down the counters and cleaned up the floors, I dropped my quarters into the slot and listened to the jazzy blues lyrics about being lonely or losing my man.

Maybe playing those sad songs was my way of languishing over Pat, my first love, or maybe I was mourning the end of my childhood freedom as I had known it. I'm not really sure what attracted me to these slow, bluesy songs. Another of my first favorite songs was the Platter's "Great Pretender." Was that me? Pretending that I'm doing well? Why was I drawn to these sad lyrics? Working was part of my life now even at this young age, and like it or not, my time was no longer my own. It was coming to light that work was not interesting or much fun. It was sad and bluesy even in the midst of bright colored lockers and a clear blue pool.

The summer finally ended and I said goodbye to the Riviera Cabana Club, lox and bagels, the jukebox and Julie London. I was eager to return to school to read and study and see my best friend, Jan. I couldn't foresee at the time that I would gradually stop studying, drop off the honor roll and barely finish school. I also couldn't foresee that I had eighteen more jobs in my future.

Job 3 Kresge's

After the long summer at the Riviera Cabana Club, I was overjoyed to be back at good old Bedford High School. I enjoyed studying and learning, but that academic happiness was short lived since it was somehow decided by my sister Betty, and this time even by my parents, that I needed to earn money to buy my own school clothes; even though I cared very little about what I wore or what was in fashion. I usually wore blue jeans and t-shirts, which was not a popular outfit for girls in the late '50s. Maybe I was ahead of my time. I had to buy the jeans in the boy's department. For school, I was required to wear skirts, blouses, or dresses, but when I was at home, I was more comfortable in a pair of jeans. Being in style did not matter one bit. In spite of that fact, I was heading back to the world of work to supposedly buy my own clothes.

Betty was friends with Geri and her sister Pauline who both worked at the lunch counter in Kresge's at Southgate Shopping Center. Pauline was nicknamed Little Bit because she was short and petite. Because of their friendship with Betty, I was recruited to work part time at the lunch counter located about two miles from our house in Warrensville Heights. In the '50s, many department stores or "five and dime" stores like F. W. Woolworths and Kresge's had these counters where tired shoppers or local businessmen could grab a quick cup of coffee or a bite to eat. The customers perched on round, chrome, cushioned stools that lined one side of a long counter. On the other side of the counter, the server dished up food and drinks.

The lunch counter at Kresge's was similar to the lunch counters that became famous for the sit-ins during the Civil Rights Movement during the '60s in the South. In the newspapers or on TV, you would see well-dressed black male and female students sitting peacefully at a "White Only" Woolworth's lunch counter in Greensboro, North Carolina waiting to be served. They sat proud and upright, facing straight forward, peacefully beseeching their equal rights. They were not served. Instead, the student dissenters were taunted, spit on, and peppered with food. When they persisted on sitting at the counter, the police forcefully dragged them from the stools and arrested them. Then, a new group of demonstrators would take their places.

Nothing this exciting was happening up North at our lunch counter. There were no Civil Rights demonstrations, but I can't honestly recall serving a black man or woman when I worked there either.

Perhaps there was some unstated segregation in the North. I'm sure that Ohio had racial issues, but not like in the South. We had no demonstrations, but we also had no African Americans at our Kresge's Five and Dime Store lunch counter. At that time in my life, though, I didn't give it a second thought.

The counter girls at Kresge's wore white uniforms with little aprons, but Little Bit's uniform was the whitest and she always had a printed hankie folded like an open flower in her breast pocket right above her name tag. I liked working with Little Bit because she was kind to me. She had a sweet, compassionate face, buck teeth and the cutest little West Virginia accent. Also, she was a fast worker who rarely stopped moving, so after the slow pace at the Cabana Club, I was forced to kick up my pace a notch just to keep up with her, but I didn't mind the busy routine.

We wore the traditional white work shoes that constantly had to be polished. The thin white shoe polish smeared over my fingers when I used the little fuzzy applicator and tried to cover over the black grime on my shoes, hoping that they would look halfway decent for the public eye. It hardly occurred to me to wash them first. My work appearance never matched up with Little Bit's crisp, clean image.

Never mind buying clothes! My main goal of working at Kresge's developed into buying every new 45 record that was ever released. For me, it was music all the way. My starting pay was $0.85 an hour

32

and I soon found out that I could buy items in the store on credit. The money would simply be deducted from my paycheck. I spent my lunch breaks flipping through the little paper covered vinyl 45 records that were organized by the name of each singer: Elvis, The Coasters, Bill Haley, Chubby Checker, Ricky Nelson, etc. The price of a 45 single was 99 cents, about the same price as a song on iTunes today, but there were two sides on a record; although, the flip side was usually not a popular hit. My very first week, I started a collection of 45 records.

At home my little square blue and white record player was in constant use. I carefully snapped a yellow disc into the middle of each 45 record to fit it on the spindle. The record dropped down, most of the time without my help, and the needle arm jerked over to the beginning of the record - music filled my room with life. I loved music and played my new records over and over again. Being poor at math, I didn't realize that it took more than an hour of my time to buy one record.

When my first payday arrived, I was excited and ran downstairs and skipped up the hallway to the little office pay window ready to collect the loot for my hard week's work. What a shock it was when I found out that my pay was overdrawn and I owed them money. The credit thing was not working out well for me. I had to slow down on buying records and get busy working to pay off my debt.

∞∞∞∞∞∞∞∞∞

20 Jobs: A Memoir

One Saturday morning, Little Bit asked me to make the orange juice. That sounds like an easy request, but keep in mind, my time in the kitchen at home was limited. First, I had to go down to the basement freezer, find the concentrate and then somehow turn that frozen mass into juice. I never made frozen orange juice before. My face red and my hands frozen as I pried, poked, prodded and did everything in my power to get the frozen concentrate out of that round can and into the pitcher, sadly to no avail. I finally gave up and went to Little Bit for help. How embarrassed can one person feel when they discover that all you do to thaw frozen juice is to run it under hot water? Embarrassed enough to remember it forever, I guess. In spite of my limited skills, Little Bit put up with me, maybe because she was friends with my sister, but probably because of her sweet personality. She never got mad when I didn't complete my counter-girl duties correctly.

Another chore I dreaded behind the lunch counter was scooping out ice cream. The chest freezer was deep and since I was short, I practically had to stand on my head to scoop out the ice cream from the huge tubs. It was rock-hard. When I made sundaes, banana splits or milkshakes, my arms were sticky clear up to my elbows. By the end of the day, it looked like a child had finger-painted a mural of chocolate and strawberry on my uniform. Needless to say, my counter work and appearance left a lot to be desired. A change was on the horizon.

G.H. Ashenfelter

The dishes we used at the Kresge's lunch counter were real solid china and had to be sent downstairs, to some unknown place, to be washed, neatly stacked and sent back upstairs. The dumbwaiter, which was a small, metal elevator, was big enough to hold several bins of dishes. A couple of weeks after I started work, I found that unknown place downstairs. I was never told why, but maybe I did not quite meet high lunch counter expectations. So, I was sent down the basement to meet up with the other end of the dumbwaiter.

Instead of being a counter server, I was henceforth the dishwasher. When the dumbwaiter arrived and the metal doors opened up, I hauled out the bus pans full of heavy, dirty china dishes, separated them into racks, rinsed them with a sprayer, and pushed them through the hot dishwashing machine. Out they came on the other side, sparkly clean. I piled them up, stacked them back on the dumbwaiter and sent the gleaming dishes upstairs to the lunch counter.

A separate little round washing machine was used to clean and sterilize the silverware. It worked well unless some stray piece of chewed-up gum was missed by the unobservant dishwasher who didn't know to check for stray gum on the silverware. As a result, what a sticky mess! It ended up that I had to scrape each individual piece of silverware to remove the hardened, glued on gum.

After that, I examined the dirty silverware more closely. I accepted my demotion and didn't really mind the work. Sometimes I felt a little lonely and missed the other servers, but washing dishes kept me busy.

Eventually, I was promoted back upstairs to waiting on customers at the lunch counter. I became more efficient with my duties and learned how to use the grill and how to make assorted sandwiches using the typical white or rye bread. Little square dishes nestled down into sections of the refrigerated cold table. These checkerboard containers were filled with tuna salad, coleslaw, egg salad, pickles, lettuce, cheese, etc. Little Bit always asked me to taste-test the egg salad, tuna, or coleslaw to make sure it wasn't spoiled. I would always comply, like getting ptomaine poisoning might be part of my job description. I gladly did whatever Little Bit asked of me. I slowly became more competent as a server, although never as competent as Little Bit.

∞∞∞∞∞∞∞∞∞∞

Once in awhile, my mom let me drive her new Buick to work since I had my temporary license. She was tired of driving me back and forth and now trusted me. A big mistake on her part!

One Sunday afternoon my mom gave me her car to drive my friend Joanie home from my house in Bedford to her house in Northfield. It was only three miles, so my mom told me to take her Buick. Like typical teens, Joanie and I were laughing, talking and paying little attention to the road ahead. I wanted to see how many boys were hanging out at the local gas station. When I took my eyes off the road and looked left at the gas station, "wham!" I crashed into something. A car had stopped in front of me to make a left turn. I didn't know that cars could stop right in the middle of the road like that. It happened fast, but at the same time everything went into slow motion, just like a scene in the movies. I saw the hood of my mom's Buick crumple up like an accordion. I did not feel or hear anything as my face slammed into the steering wheel. Stunned and in shock, I looked over at Joanie. She had hit the windshield and her face was covered with blood. That really scared me.

I don't remember who called my dad, maybe I did. When he arrived his face was red and twisted up in anger. There were people, police cars and flashing lights everywhere. Dad's first words to me were, "You did all this?" Looking around for the first time, I realized that the car I hit had been pushed in front of an oncoming car, so it was a three car pile-up. Yes, I did all this and I felt awful. My stomach was tied in knots and my head hung down in shame. I couldn't even look at or talk to my dad when he drove us to the hospital. Even though Joanie had lots of blood on her face, her cuts were superficial, and to my relief, she was fine. By this time my face was swollen up flat with two evenly matched black eyes. I deserved it, I thought to myself. "You should know better," the parental refrain echoed in my ears.

∞∞∞∞∞∞∞∞∞

Working at Kresge's I didn't use Latin or algebra or any of the subjects that were taught in my college prep courses at high school, so after my car accident I decided to change from college prep classes to business classes. When I was on the Honor Roll, the counselors and my parents had talked to me about going on to college, but as a working girl, I could no longer picture myself pursuing higher education. None of my family had attended college and it looked like I wouldn't either.

In fact, I almost didn't graduate from high school. That is a whole other story - my best friend, Jan, and I discovered the joys of skipping school. Since we both had part time jobs and a little money in our pockets, it was very easy. Jan was a thin, petite blonde with a sense of adventure. We always had fun together, and best of all, she had a driver's license. Jan and I were high-spirited and carefree like many teens at seventeen. Sure we had problems in our lives, her parents drank too much and so did my mom. In fact, my parents were on the verge of getting a divorce. But when we were together, none of this mattered. We just had fun. School didn't fall into the fun category, so we started skipping it on a regular basis. It was all so easy. Jan drove her uncle's 1958 Buick to school and picked me up each morning. We flipped a coin to decide whether to go to school or to go to Geneva on the Lake. If the coin landed in our favor, fine, if not, we flipped it two out of three times. This manipulation of fate usually worked and we headed off to Geneva. The next day we wrote fake notes and forged our moms' names for Mrs. Kyle the truant officer. At that time there was no strict attendance policy - by March, we had missed about fifty days of school.

Unfortunately, our vagrant ways finally caught up with us. One afternoon after our usual fun day of skipping school, Jan called home and her mom was furious. The school found out we were skipping and contacted our parents. I could tell by the look on Jan's face that we were in big trouble. In our under-developed teen minds it only made sense that we should flee to New Orleans for Mardi Gras. We never made it home from school that evening. We ran away from home but never made it to New Orleans. We only got as far as Tennessee. It's a long story, but it did have a happy ending. We both graduated from Bedford High School - me by the skin of my teeth with a D in Government.

Jan and I remained friends throughout the years. She became an operating room nurse at Metro Hospital in Cleveland and I became . . . well keep reading and you'll find out. Many times we looked back at our adventures and wondered what we were thinking, or if we were thinking at all. The only thing we could come up with was that we just wanted to have fun. After that major drama, I was ready to move on with my life. No more running away for me. It was time to grow up.

Gladys & Jan at graduation

Job 4 - The Stencil Factory

It is 1961 and I'm a new graduate of Bedford High School. It felt strange being out of high school and somewhat unsettling. For one thing, there were no more carefree days with my friend Jan, riding around in her uncle's car and skipping school. Time to join the real world of work, as everyone liked to say, even though I had already worked for four years.

In my real world after high school, I was dating a steady boyfriend named Earl whom I had met through his sister Nancy. He was nice looking and tall, about six feet, with blue eyes and blond hair. Earl had been discharged from the Army after serving time as a paratrooper in the 101st Airborne. He had been stationed in Seoul where he guarded the border between North and South Korea. He was in great shape and sported the current sharp-looking crew cut hair style, which was combed straight up to form a little wall above his forehead. I liked his looks but didn't fall madly in love with him like I had for Pat when I was fourteen. It was more the idea of having a boyfriend that appealed to me, especially one that had traveled the world and jumped out of airplanes. At my age, it was the norm for girls to date and be in a relationship, and so I was.

After graduation, for some strange reason, Betty didn't have a job lined up for me, but thanks to the shift from college classes to business classes, I could type and do shorthand. I decided to look for a position as a secretary in an office. This was the 1960s, before the Internet, and the best way to find a job was to look through the ads in the *Cleveland Press* or *Cleveland Plain Dealer* newspapers. I spread out the newspaper on the living room floor, took a pencil and carefully circled the phone numbers to call for nearby office positions. The ads were separated into two help wanted categories – "Help Wanted Female" or "Help Wanted Male." Under female you could find more categories like Nursing, Office Help, Teacher or Waitress. Imagine work being classified as male or female today. Maybe jobs are not divided by gender today, but if you look, there is still a distinct division in job opportunities.

At that time I had no idea about equality for women or the Nineteenth Amendment that was passed in the year 1920 giving women the right to vote. Women fought 70 years for this unprecedented voting privilege. This fight for equality and the right to vote was termed "the first wave of feminism." After that, the Equal Rights Amendment, ERA, was introduced into every Congress starting in 1923. The ERA, that affirmed the equal application of the Constitution to all persons regardless of their sex, was written in 1923 by Alice Paul, suffragist leader and founder of the National Woman's Party. She promoted the ERA as the next step in confirming "equal justice under law" for all citizens.

The Equal Rights Amendment passed the Senate in 1972, by a margin vote of one. Then, it was sent to the states for ratification. It was confirmed by 35 states, but fell short by three states for the required 38 states for the bill to be fully ratified. Today it is still not in the Constitution. In 1961, I was far from being an independent woman in the workplace. Basically I did whatever I was told to do, like many women in my generation. I accepted whatever pay was offered and didn't expect the same pay that a man earned. Never ever would I dare to ask for a raise or a higher starting pay. Even today, I don't think I would have the nerve to do that.

After sending applications by mail and interviewing at a few small business places, I was hired at a stencil book factory that was located on Broadway around the corner from my house on Magnolia Street. I don't remember the name of the place, maybe Bedford Stencil Company, but, not sure. I needed a job close by because I lost my driver's license after the accident with my mother's Buick. With no car and no driver's license, I simply walked around the corner to begin my first day of work at the stencil factory.

20 Jobs: A Memoir

The boss lady who ran the company gave me the nickname of Cookie, which I found out later was her name for every new secretary. I don't remember her name, but she was a tiny, trim and fashionable older woman. She walked me through my new secretarial duties of typing up invoices and sorting mail. The tasks were not difficult, and I caught on easily to the routine. I wasn't even sure it could be called work, compared to running on my feet all day waiting on customers at Kresge's, this was the gravy train. Feeling important in my new office, I sat up straight in my cushioned chair in front of the shiny, black Underwood typewriter. I typed out invoices and answered the phone in my new business voice. Thanks to my high school business courses, I was prepared to tackle any paperwork or typing job coming my way.

A skill that proved invaluable was typing. When I was in middle school, I taught myself to type on our old, black Underwood typewriter using Betty's barely used, red typing book. I sat at our kitchen table and folded the book back so it would stand up like a big V and started from the beginning page. I liked the clicking sound and the feel of punching those black keys down that made a lever fly up and strike a ribbon. Letters appeared on the paper: gf gf hj hj asdf jkl. At the end of each line a bell would ring, and then I reached up with my left hand to push the little shiny lever and throw the carriage back to the beginning of the next line.

G.H. Ashenfelter

Typing in the early '60s was highly interactive and far different from our modern word processing. It could be compared to cooking on an old fashioned wood burning stove instead of cooking on a modern range. On the wood burning stove, you threw in the wood, coaxed up the fire and waited patiently. Today, on a modern range, you turn a knob to start the burner. On the typewriter, it required patience as you rolled in a sheet of paper and positioned it at a starting point. The margins were manually set with little metal tabs before you began to type. Then the typist pushed down hard on the keys and tried not to make a mistake, which required going back and whiting out each letter that was wrong and retyping the correct letter in its place. Today, on modern computers, we select our margins and begin to type - it's so easy to just hit "delete" to fix any error without touching messy black ribbons or using Liquid Paper, which is now Wite-Out, to fix a mistake. Thanks to my persistent practice with typing, I was able to carry out my office duties and make the boss lady proud.

If the office work was slow, and many times it was, my boss directed me to the back production room where I helped assemble the stencil books. I found this boring as I sat for hours and put pages together to form the books that were later bound with spiral plastic rings before they were shipped out. The stencil books were mainly for children and featured plants, animals and flower shapes. Before computers and video games, these books were a popular form of entertainment for kids who would carefully trace these shapes onto paper. I remember, because I was one of those kids. You can still find stencil books in stores today, but most likely they are purchased by adults who fondly remember them from their childhood days.

∞∞∞∞∞∞∞∞∞

I had a dilemma that interfered with my work. The boredom of office work and doing the same thing over and over didn't keep me busy enough and gave me too much time to think. My mind wandered off as I constantly imagined what my steady boyfriend, Earl, might be up to. He worked second shift while I worked days. As I sat typing or assembling stencil books, in my mind's eye, plain as day, I saw my boyfriend cruising in his white Buick right by Northfield High School at lunch time, looking cool and probably picking up that skank, Judy, my arch-rival and Earl's ex-girlfriend. It became difficult to concentrate on my office duties, so I started taking time off work to "check up" on the whereabouts of the wandering Casanova.

One day I skipped work, borrowed a car and drove up by the high school. Right away I spotted Earl's white Buick and my pulse quickened when I saw a girl sitting next to him. I pulled up by his car, jumped out and yanked open the passenger door, ready to fight. Imagine my surprise when I saw his sister Linda sitting there instead of my imaginary foe. We looked at each other and burst out laughing. Years later Linda told me that she really was scared when she saw my eyes, black lined with mascara and full of fire. Linda and I remain friends to this day.

Along with my jealousy, it didn't help that I stayed up late at night waiting for Earl to get off his job at midnight so we could spend more time together. We would sit in his car in front of my house for hours and it was often two or three in the morning before I got to bed. These late nights and distracted thinking were hazardous to my work.

The sleepy mornings and skipped work days ended my job at the stencil factory. Who knows, it may have led to a secure future. After all, I was the favorite Cookie of the day. Before this office job, I considered myself a dependable worker, but to my dismay, I had lost this office position due to my poor working habits. Deep down it bothered me because my family stressed how important it was to "do your best in a job." Relationships can get in the way of even the best of careers. In defense of losing my job, I reasoned that I was used to a more active work environment and it was monotonous for me sit still all day in one spot. Little did I know, that is exactly what I would be doing in some future jobs, but I'm getting ahead of the story.

Job 5 Kresge's # 2

By the time I started my fifth job, I was officially in a relationship with my boyfriend Earl. This was partly due to the fact that I neglected my fourth job as a secretary in favor of pursuing what I thought was a grand romance. Thinking back, I am not so sure that I was in love, but I was in love with the idea of being in love. Unfortunately, since I lost the job at the stencil factory I had to find new employment.

Drawing on my prior experience as a counter girl at Kresge's in Southgate, I easily found a job at a different Kresge's located in Northfield Plaza in Northfield Village, close to where Earl lived. I feel it's fair to count this Kresge's in Northfield as a separate job, since it was a new location and the work was somewhat different. I didn't own a vehicle, due to the accident with my mother's car, so my boyfriend Earl drove me to work or I caught a ride with a co-worker. I was now nineteen.

G.H. Ashenfelter

During the week, I did the usual counter work like at I did at Southgate, but on the weekends I turned into Super-Sub Girl. On Saturday mornings, I arrived at the store early to start preparing the famous fresh deli submarines or hoagies, as they were also called. These subs were filled with three kinds of meat: ham, bologna, and salami, freshly sliced on an electric slicer by me – Super-Sub Girl. Along with the meat, they contained cheese, lettuce, peppers, tomatoes and onions thinly sliced, also by me, and stacked in a hoagie bun spread with yellow mustard. This delicious perfection was prepared with extra care by, yes; you guessed it - Super-Sub Girl.

When a customer walked in the front door of Kresge's, they were greeted by a large sign that read, "Subs for sale, three for a dollar!" Maybe it was a sense of pride in making a delicious, popular sandwich or maybe it was because it was the end of the week, but whatever the reason, I looked forward to preparing these fresh subs each Saturday. I had gained a reputation, and also a few pounds, by making the best hoagies in town and had many regular customers. This made me feel important in an ordinary sort of way. Because, I thought, who couldn't make a sub sandwich? Still, for the first time ever, I was working independently and was my own boss even if it was for making subs. I wasn't following others around trying to be like them because I had my own little niche as number one Super-Sub Girl.

After making submarines all day, I carefully prepared three special ones with extra meat and cheese to set aside for my date with Earl on Saturday night. Our typical date was going to the outdoor drive-in theatre that was right next door to the Kresge's Plaza. At closing time, Earl would be waiting by the door in his shiny white Buick and I would happily dash out to the car carrying the white paper bag bulging with the extra-special subs. If we didn't have enough money, as was often the case, we sat in the plaza parking lot next door to the drive-in where we could see the big screen, but heard no sound from the movie. Sad to say, he was bad with money and I was a cheap date! What we did hear instead of the movie was the rustle of the paper wrappers and loud chewing as we devoured our tasty hoagies made by . . . oh, you know who.

Other fond memories of working at Kresge's were meeting new people and the interaction with customers and co-workers. One day, while working the counter, I waited on a lovely, blonde girl about 21. She sat down and I was struck by her friendly personality. I asked her name and she replied that her name was Candy. I commented about how the name fit her and how much I liked it. She then confessed that it was not her real name, her real name was Earlene. At first I thought, what a strange name, but then another thought occurred to me. What if my first child was a girl? I could name her Earlene after this lovely young lady. It seemed like a wonderful idea since my boyfriend was named Earl. But why was I even thinking about babies at this time?

I wonder if I had marriage on my mind, because one night I dreamed a vivid dream about a wedding, mine in fact, and the groom was Earl. When I woke up, this dream did not fade away from my memory like most dreams. It still felt as real as it did when I was asleep. I couldn't shake the memory. Premonitions or dreams can sometimes come true.

∞∞∞∞∞∞∞∞∞∞

I don't remember Earl specifically asking me to marry him, but I ended up with the engagement ring on my finger shortly after that dream. Events snowballed out of my control. We were visiting Earl's mom, Mildred, and sipping on root beer floats. Suddenly mine slipped from my hand and rolled across the living room rug.

"Oh, I'm sorry." I burst out as my face reddened.

"It's alright, dear," said Mildred as she grabbed up the rolling glass and left the room to make me another float. When she came back she had a new float and something else in her other hand; a small box. I eyed it nervously as Earl's mom made a big show of showing us the rings that belonged to his grandmother, Grandma Frye. The box contained a plain gold band and a ring with one clear white stone. Suddenly it was official; I was engaged.

Next was a bridal shower, also planned and given by Mildred, complete with her famous strawberry glaze pies. Most of the shower guests were her friends except for my two sisters, Betty and Jane, my mom and my best friend Barbie. Jan was busy pursuing her education to become a nurse, so she was not there.

When it was time to pick the location for the wedding, I still had no voice. Based on Mildred's plans, Earl and I were to be married at a preacher's study in Akron. Of course the preacher, chosen by Mildred, was an old family acquaintance. It would be a small wedding, no bridesmaids or friends, only family. I wanted to invite my friends, but it did not seem to be an option - not enough room, not enough money. Not sure why, but maybe it was partly my fault for not speaking out. Our wedding was being planned by my future mother-in-law. I went along with the plans, unable to resist, like a tide pulled by the moon or a dream premonition played out in real life.

Looking back, I'm not sure why my family didn't help plan the wedding since that was the tradition. Probably it was because my mom and dad were newly divorced and things were not going well in our family. Maybe they felt it was best to let Mildred do the planning. Whatever the reason, the big life changing event came true just like my dream.

∞∞∞∞∞∞∞∞∞∞

G.H. Ashenfelter

I remember the day well. It was June 30th, 1962, a hot, muggy summer day. The chapel was not air conditioned and I felt sweat trickle down the back of my white lace wedding dress. I walked hesitantly into the preacher's study accompanied by a record player scratching out "Here Comes the Bride." My mid-calf length dress felt stiff, unnatural and scratchy; my bouquet was shaking ever so slightly and it started to pour rain outside, a quick summer downpour. I felt strange; the air was so close. Standing up front in the small room, I smelled that the preacher had bad breath and it made me feel nauseous. I glanced up at Earl for a look of reassurance, but he wouldn't look at me. He was standing stiffly in his dark suit and tie staring straight ahead. No help there. He looked like he was at a funeral, pale as a sheet and ready to pass out cold.

When I saw how scared he looked, I got a feeling of dread. This was supposed to be a happy day, but it looked like Earl didn't really wish to get married and suddenly I wasn't sure that I did either. I bit my lip, but it didn't help, tears rolled silently down my cheeks. Unable to stop, I cried through the whole ceremony. What were we doing? Too late! The ceremony ended and we were married for better or for worse, thanks to my mother-in-law who gave us the ring, the bridal shower and finally the wedding. It was a done deal.

After the ceremony, the feeling of dread passed. Earl and I drove up to New York State and honeymooned at Niagara Falls. It was a miserable ride up - the car was stinking hot and had no air conditioning, which was found only in high-end cars in those days. I don't remember seeing Niagara Falls, but I suppose we did. After that, we drove to upstate New York to visit my mom's relatives. My cousins liked my new husband, he teased the girls and they got along great. When I saw Earl with my New York family, I felt better about being married.

Back from our honeymoon, Earl moved into my house on Magnolia Street in Bedford, but living there with my family wasn't working out and we realized that we wanted to have a place of our own. Thanks to a suggestion from friends, we found and bought a little house on land contract that was located in Red Fox development in Shalersville Township. The tiny, three bedroom slab house cost $9,500 and our house payments were $79 a month. We could afford that with Earl's aluminum factory job. It was exciting to own a home and at that point I felt happy to be married.

I continued working at Kresge's for a while longer. We bought a bedroom set, an older ornate bed, dresser and dressing table, from a co-worker - the big old dresser from that set still remains with me today. We settled into our new little house. Not long after we moved to Red Fox, a neighbor helped Earl get a better paying job at US Steel and Wire in Cleveland. I no longer needed to work at Kresge's. We reasoned that I didn't earn much money anyhow, so I quit my job to concentrate on being a housewife.

Job 6, Kenny Kings

Cleaning up the slab, ticky-tacky house on the hillside didn't take much time and I was soon bored with staying home. Phone calls were expensive unless I was calling a local number, no unlimited calling in the early '60s. Out in Red Fox in Shalersville, not many numbers were local. Friends and relatives seemed far away and I felt out of touch. Newly married and living out in the suburbs, way out, my days were lonely and quiet when my husband was working, and to be honest, not that exciting when he wasn't.

Earl was a quiet man and I discovered that we really didn't have much to talk about. To be fair, he was exhausted from working in the hot steel mills; his job was not easy. He ate dinner, slept and went back to work. The boredom may have been part of the reason I decided to seek another job. I'm not sure how I found it, but I started my sixth job working at Kenny Kings Restaurant on Columbus Road in Bedford. A carhop again! Is my life going around in circles?   This time though, the excitement of waiting on cars and making tips was gone.

It felt entirely different being a carhop at twenty than it did when I was fourteen and working at Ginny's. One main reason was insecurity about my looks. My teeth were missing fillings in the front and in desperate need of repair. That really bothered me. There was no fluoride in the water when I was growing up; plus I chewed a lot of bubble gum as a kid, so buying that penny candy at the corner store had caught up with me. My mom took me to the dentist and I remember sitting for long hours in misery as he worked on filling my teeth. No painless dentistry back then, but I was taught to be stoic - no babies in our family. "Stop crying! You're fine" was our family motto. But my fillings had fallen out and my teeth were full of holes, so I barely opened my mouth to smile. Embarrassed for my looks, I held my hand up to cover my mouth as I talked and now disliked working in the public.

∞∞∞∞∞∞∞∞∞

Fast-food was making a speedy entrance into the American landscape, and here I was working at the fast-food restaurant of the famous Colonel Harland Sanders featuring his Kentucky Fried Chicken. Kentucky Fried Chicken was advertised as being "finger-lickin' good!" And it was! The chicken was heavily breaded, cooked to a crisp, golden brown and served up in a bucket with hot, fresh crispy fries, rolls and creamy home-made coleslaw on the side. Americans were in love with this chicken dinner and I couldn't blame them. It smelled like heaven and tasted mouth-watering delicious!

As I solemnly waited on the cars with my half-hidden smile, I was not aware of the history behind the distinguished looking Colonel Harland Sanders whose image graced our signs and chicken buckets. He was an icon with his snowy white hair, moustache and goatee, looking just like a distinguished old southern gentleman. There was an amazing story behind that image.

Harland David Sanders was born in 1890 in Henryville, Indiana. By the time he was 40, Sanders was running a popular Kentucky service station that also served food. As his reputation grew, he moved across the street from his service station and opened a motel and restaurant that seated 142 people. It was here where he perfected his secret blend of 11 herbs and spices along with the basic cooking technique that is still used today. The governor of Kentucky designated him a Kentucky colonel. The company went on to become the world's largest fast-food chicken chain, Kentucky Fried Chicken. His famous Kentucky fried chicken can still be found today under the KFC logo.

To continue Colonel Sander's story, when he was confident of the quality of his fried chicken at his restaurant, the Colonel then devoted himself to the chicken franchising business. In 1952, he traveled across the country by car from restaurant to restaurant, cooking batches of chicken for restaurant owners and their employees. If the reaction was favorable, he entered into a handshake agreement on a deal that stipulated a payment to him of a nickel for each piece of chicken the restaurant sold.

By 1964, Colonel Sanders had more than 600 franchised outlets for his chicken in the United States and Canada. In 20 years, the chain grew to 18 units in northern Ohio earning in excess of $5.5 million a year. Even today, who doesn't like Kentucky Fried Chicken and who doesn't admire a man who worked so hard for his success?

Before his fame, Harland Sanders had many work experiences: a cook for his family, a farm worker, a streetcar conductor at age 15, a soldier in Cuba, a railroad fireman, a law student, an insurance salesman, a steamboat ferry operator on the Ohio River, a tire salesman and a service station operator. Who knows, maybe he had more jobs than I had.

I was not aware of this information about Colonel Sanders at the time I worked at Kenny Kings. I just saw his picture everywhere, considered it an advertisement and never gave a second thought about the fact that he was a real person. Now I can appreciate his style and ambition, but at that time, I didn't care. I was wrapped up in my new status as a married woman and worried about my smile. I only stayed on the job as a carhop at this famous restaurant for a couple of months.

Some chapters or jobs in life are short lived. Working at Kenny Kings is one of these chapters. Thinking back, I remember that my husband Earl didn't like it when I worked. The traditional household scenario in the '60s was that the man worked and the woman stayed home to cook and keep up with the household chores. After Kenny Kings, I was back in my little slab house, feeling isolated, I was not sure how to handle being a wife. It was a transition time from being single, carefree and working to being married, responsible and stuck at home. Somehow, working as a carhop did not fit me anymore, yet being a wife didn't fit either.

Job 7- Howard Johnson's

Isolated out in the rural development of Red Fox, I often wished that I still worked. There was nothing for me to do but clean or cook. I quickly discovered that these were not my favorite activities and I wasn't a good cook at all. When I first got married, I could only make grilled cheese sandwiches, peanut butter cookies and of course submarine sandwiches. Often I served undercooked chicken and lumpy potatoes. In fact, my husband Earl lost 20 pounds soon after we were married. In direct contrast, my mother-in-law Mildred was a great cook and made hearty Pennsylvania Dutch dishes like pies, dumplings, stews and chicken pot pie.

Mildred worried about her son losing so much weight and decided to teach me to cook. I complied and eventually became a decent cook. Even so, I was increasingly bored being at home, most of the time alone. Up to this point in my life, I had lived with my family in the town of Bedford with movies, libraries, parks and stores close by. Around the housing development there were only other houses just like mine, the gravel pit and a little county cemetery. I needed something else to occupy up my time.

As if in answer to my prayers, my best friend Barbie contacted me about a job opening for waitresses at Howard Johnson's Restaurant on Northfield Road in Warrensville Heights. We applied together and each got a waitress position for evenings and weekends. Barbie and I were friends since our childhood and I was excited to get the chance to be with her again.

Growing up, Barbie lived right around the corner from me in Bedford. She was an only child, thin built with brown eyes, curly blonde hair and enough energy to run a power plant. Although she was closer to Betty's age, she did not like Betty and did not want to hang around with her. Instead, Barbie adopted me as her little sister. How fortunate for me that Barbie picked me as her friend! She had a sunny disposition and patiently taught me many childhood skills, including how to ride a bike.

Barbie informed me, "You can't fall over when riding your bike down a hill." I believed her. I can't fall, I told myself, even though I was scared. I sat at the top of the hill looking down at the road and trusted in her words. I pushed off a little shaky, but was soon flying down the slope and keeping my balance. It worked. I could ride a bike.

That was only the beginning of the many fun things Barbie taught me. She taught me to play jacks, badminton and hopscotch. We tap danced on the sidewalk and jumped double-dutch in the street using two jump ropes. On summer mornings, Barbie came up to my messy room and dragged me out of the tangled bed sheets to take long walks by the river on paths in the Bedford Glens. We hiked along the railroad tracks and picked wild strawberries, so tiny and sweet, that grew out of the coal cinders. Life with Barbie was never boring.

Barbie's house sat about ten feet away from the railroad tracks, so when a big steam engine rolled by, her house shook in unison to the rumble of the giant wheels on the tracks. You couldn't hear a thing until the train passed. One night we were watching Elvis on the Ed Sullivan Show when a train roared by. It didn't matter because we were screaming so loudly we couldn't hear the train or Elvis. I loved spending time with Barbie. We grew up together in the same neighborhood and now here we were, both married and working together at Howard Johnson's.

Having a job again and working with my friend Barbie gave me back some freedom plus the chance to earn a little extra spending money. We often rode to work together and laughed merrily like we were kids again. Looking back, we really were. Another plus was that after going to an oral surgeon and getting my upper teeth pulled and a plate put in, I didn't mind working with the public and could smile again. It was upsetting and traumatic for me to lose my teeth when I was so young, but at that time, it was a necessity. Being very vain, I never, ever let anyone see me without my plate, but I had my smile back - and I had my friend back by my side.

Since the age of the automobile was in full swing, Americans were on the move and the travelers could easily spot the white colonial style building with a bright orange roof topped with a white cupola. Out front the large orange and blue Howard Johnson's sign advertised the 28 flavors of ice cream. Inside the restaurant, weary families could sit down and order tasty hot food and choose from assorted pies and flavors of ice cream for dessert. Howard Johnson's was the largest food chain in the United States throughout the 1960s and 1970s.

This was another success story for a 20th century entrepreneur, Howard Deering Johnson. In 1961, Howard Johnson's Company went public. There were 605 restaurants, 265 company-owned and 340 franchised, as well as 88 franchised Howard Johnson's motor lodges in 32 states. Howard Johnson's trademark orange roof and pie man weathervane were a welcome and familiar sight, much like McDonald's golden arches are to travelers today. Again, I was not aware of this information. To me this restaurant was only a place to work.

I liked the idea of being a real table waitress, not just a counter girl or carhop like at Kresge's and Kenny Kings. Howard Johnson waitresses wore starched, crisply ironed, orange and blue uniforms with a little white apron tied neatly around their waists and pinned into a perfect bow in the back. We also wore little hats and hair nets. Every afternoon before our shift started the manager conducted a waitress inspection. We lined up as he checked our shoes, which had to be a certain brand, white and polished. Then he checked our hands and nails. Last of all, he made us turn around so he could see the bow on our aprons to make sure it was tied perfectly straight. At least that is what he was supposed to be looking at. Hard to imagine this type of scrutiny for a waitress job nowadays, but that was how it was back then. I took this inspection very seriously and spent lots of time getting ready to go to work and serve the public fried clam strips and 28 flavors of ice cream.

One Sunday afternoon while I was working the back section at Howard Johnson's, a group of four teenage boys came in and sat in one of my big booths. I walked up smiling my now perfect smile, pen and pad in hand, ready to take their order. The teens ordered the most expensive steaks on the menu. I raised my eyebrows and hesitated at this request, but then went ahead and wrote down the order. Can you hear "gullible" in your head? The boys were smiling and laughing when the steaks came out of the kitchen. In a short amount of time, the food was devoured, so I placed their checks on the table. Then I walked up front, but when I came back to collect the money, my eyes scanned the empty booth and my mouth flew open wide just like the back door emergency exit. Oh no! They had pulled a fast one on me.

It was company policy at Howard Johnson's, as in many restaurants, that waitresses were responsible for the check if it didn't get paid, so it took all my tips and more to settle that debt for four choice steak dinners. Many restaurants still have that policy. If a waitress chases a customer out the door because they accidentally forgot to pay the check, now you know why. If they don't pay it, she might be forced to foot the bill.

I learned some life lessons from working at Ho Jo's, as we so fondly called it. I learned to watch out for sneaky teens who sit close to a back door. Along with that, I learned how to tie a perfect apron bow and how much I liked fried clams. My part-time employment only lasted maybe three to six months. When it was over, I missed my free time away from the house, but most of all I missed my time with Barbie.

∞∞∞∞∞∞∞∞∞∞

Barbie and her husband Tom had two children in two years, a girl and a boy, and soon after that, a set of twins, a boy and a girl - four kids in three years. Not long after Barbie left Howard Johnson's, she changed her destiny. She decided to take her four babies and move to southern Ohio where the cost of living was cheaper and she could live closer to her grandmother. She didn't ask permission from her husband or care what he thought about moving. She just took her babies, went down to Uhrichsville, bought a house and moved in. Her husband Tom eventually followed along and from there he got a job working on the railroad. One thing about Barbie, she was an independent woman before her time. I could have taken some lessons from her in that department.

It wasn't too long after I left Howard Johnson's that I became pregnant with our first child. On an early Wednesday morning, June 13th, 1963, my little girl was born. As predicted, I named her Earlene Renae, after the lovely blonde girl I met at Kresge's. It was not an easy labor. The morning before, when my labor first started, Earl decided he should go to work and I should go over to his mother's house to spend the day and be closer to the hospital in Warrensville Heights. We needed the money after all. Having no choice, I agreed. But I felt like he was deserting me and I was not happy about it at all.

My mother-in-law Mildred did take good care of me though and served up delicious creamed asparagus on toast for dinner, which came back up later that night at the hospital, not so tasty. After about 24 hours of labor, Earlene came into the world, face up instead of face down, a type of breach. My next two babies would do the same.

The next day I was not pleased when Earl took the day off work to run around and tell his friends that he was a new dad. What happened to "we need the money?" I stewed over the fact that he left me with his mother while I was in labor and then took off the next day when I was stuck at the hospital. Oh, well, nothing I could do about it.

∞∞∞∞∞∞∞∞∞∞

G.H. Ashenfelter

Ten and a half months later, my second little girl, Amber Lynn, was born. She arrived during the afternoon on Tuesday, May 7th, and I named her after a character in the historical romance book *Forever Amber*. The Amber in the book was the mistress to the king of France. The labor was shorter this time and the neighbor drove me to Brentwood Hospital because Earl was at work. We could not reach him right away.

I went through labor and delivery alone, well the doctors were there, but no husband. Maybe to help me feel better, the doctors asked if I wanted to watch the birth of the baby. At first I thought, no, but then changed my mind. I'm glad I did when I saw the miracle of my second little girl born into the world reflected in a round mirror above the doctors' heads. I felt detached like it was movie and really wasn't me, but it was me alright. And now I had a second daughter.

After the delivery, my bed was moved out in the hallway because there were no rooms available. What a day this was turning out to be, I thought. Suddenly I recognized my dad's voice asking for me. "I'm right here, Dad!" I mumbled groggily as I tried to sit up. He heard me and laughed when he saw that I was parked on a bed out in the hall. I was happy to see him. I felt blue after having the baby all alone, but was trying to be brave - now Dad was here and it was fine.

A little later, Earl came to the hospital and brought me a huge bouquet of lilacs from his mother's bushes. I accepted them gratefully since I loved lilacs. My hurt feelings were forgotten. It never fails that on May 7th the lilacs bloom in Ohio and I relive the day Amber was born.

With major responsibilities at home, taking care of a house and two little baby girls, there was no time to be bored. This was the beginning of my realization that life is not just about me. It was about making sure my two babies were clean and fed, over and over again. While the girls napped, I perched on the edge of the couch, folded diapers and watched soap operas or Mike Douglas on a black and white TV. No more working outside of the house for me. My main duties were endless laundry, fixing bottles and folding cloth diapers for hours, only to do the same thing the next day and the next, along with taking care of a husband and two babies.

Disposable diapers were a future luxury. Moms today would be grossed out to know that back then soiled diapers were rinsed out in the toilet and soaked in an enamel diaper pail full of bleach water. Then the whole smelly mess was dumped into the washer and put on spin cycle. Next, they were rinsed in cold water, spun again and finally washed in hot, hot water with Dreft to kill any germs. Not a fun activity for sure. I was greatly beholden to our washer and dryer.

Looking back at myself as a young mom, I try to remember if I was happy or not. I do remember being busy, but often lonely for adult company since

Earl worked long hours and long distance phone calls were expensive. Red Fox was an island of pre-fab houses built out in the middle of nowhere. I eventually made friends with the neighbors to save my sanity. I needed to talk to an adult or run the risk of going to the loony bin. Finally, a little Save 4 Store was built on ST RT 303 within walking distance of our house. Now I had someplace to go if we needed bread, milk or gasoline. A trip to the store was an exciting event in my little corner of the Red Fox world.

I don't mean this to sound like taking care of kids was total drudgery; it wasn't. I loved my children and enjoyed them immensely, most of the time. I didn't really have the advance training to be a proper mom. I was unprepared for the endless responsibility that went along with taking care of a house and two baby girls under the age of two. It was an unpleasant surprise, even a shock to me, that my life was no longer my own. Before having kids, I had lots time by myself to read and relax. As a teen I spent hours sitting, studying and reading. My family, especially Betty, called me lazy when I sat and read a book, but I would ignore them and just keep reading. With two babies, that free time to read or relax became a luxury of the past and I missed it!

∞∞∞∞∞∞∞∞∞∞

Staying in the spirit of this book, I don't count housewife or motherhood as one of my jobs, since they were not paid positions or even considered real jobs in those days, even though being a housewife and mother is a full time job and even more.

G.H. Ashenfelter

Job 8 - Northfield Race Track

The days were continuous like the spin cycle of our washing machine. My husband Earl, my two little girls, Earlene and Amber and I continued to live out in Red Fox homes. My daily life consisted of laundry, housework and TV. Tired of the isolation, I was secretly delighted when my sister Betty suggested that I apply for a part time job as a waitress at Northfield Race Track. Betty constantly bragged about how much money she made in tips as a clubhouse waitress at the track, sometimes as much as $100 a night. That was a lot of money back then. It seemed like an eternity since I had left my house for any length of time or did much of anything except change, wash, and fold diapers. I jumped at the chance to go back to work. My husband, Earl, grudgingly agreed that money was tight, so my working a part time job would help that situation.

This position at the race track was unlike any server position that I worked in the past. Even though it was another waitress job, a clubhouse waitress was definitely more high class than working at Howard Johnsons or behind a lunch counter at Kresge's. For the first time ever, I would be serving beer, liquor, prime rib and seafood - not hamburgers, French fries and milkshakes. Other than that, I had no idea what to expect, but I was eager to try my hand at something new.

Northfield Racetrack had humble beginnings. Built back in 1934, it was intended for greyhound racing and called Sportsman Park. When this original plan eventually failed, it was sold and became a midget car racing facility. This was popular until the '50s when public interest in car racing began to subside. In 1956, Sportsman Park was demolished and the premier harness racing track, Northfield Park, was built. Northfield Park was opened in 1957 by Grandview Race Track's owner, Walter J. Michael, owner of Pickwick Farms, Ohio's most prominent standardbred breeding farm. He also owned a stable of notable horses including Miss Gene Abbe, the equine star of the motion picture, *Home in Indiana*. Because of Michael's vision to expand the racing season, Northfield Park was one of the most popular attractions in our area when I began working there in 1965.

On my first night of work, I remember pulling my car into the huge gravel parking lot in front of a long rectangle building with NORTHFIELD PARK printed in large, block letters on the outside wall. It was massive, but not ornate. It looked similar to a large factory. I sat for a minute, then got out of my car and walked with hesitant steps toward the looming giant wall, trying to calm the flutters in my stomach while searching for an entrance in this gigantic building. Where is the right door? Where am I supposed to go in? I mumbled to myself.

Luckily, I spotted another waitress wearing a black skirt, white blouse, and black vest just like me, so I speeded up and followed her through an unmarked doorway and up some dingy concrete steps. At the top of the steps, a glass door opened up, to my surprise, into a sweeping panorama of formal, white table tops. To the right, floor to ceiling, windows overlooked the half mile race track that stretched out as far as the eye could see. The immensity of it all made me feel a little disoriented. My world up to this point was made of smaller living and working spaces, little houses, small diners and family restaurants. I had that feeling that I was no longer in black and white Kansas, but was now in the Technicolor Emerald City of racing.

To get back my sense of reality, I looked around anxiously for my sister Betty. With relief, I spotted her working and carefully placing stemmed water glasses on tables topped with starched, white linens. Betty looked up and waved. I hurried towards her and she seemed happy to see her little sister and immediately took me under her wing.

"I'm here," I mumbled as I brushed back my hair.

"About time! You have to set up your tables, follow me." She said and gave me a half smile.

Betty led me into the kitchen to find the schedule that noted where my waitress station would be that night. It was down along the windows. Next, she led me to where the white linen tablecloths were stored. We grabbed an armful and proceeded down the steps to the window station and dressed up the table tops in white. Betty showed me the proper way to arrange the heavy silverware, which we double cleaned and shined up with soda water to remove any spots left from the dishwasher. The next lesson was how to fold the fancy burgundy cloth napkins so they stood up in a perfect V on the tables. This took some practice and my napkins kind of sagged in the middle. The goblet water glasses were inspected for spots or lipstick stains and set upside down in place above the knife. My sister was surprisingly patient in the role of a teacher as she walked me through the routine of setting up. Thus began my education as a racetrack waitress.

After setting up the tables in our stations, before the clubhouse opened, the waitresses had time to take a break and eat supper. That was a perk, a free meal before the customers arrived. It was always tasty, sometimes leftover cordon bleu or prime rib if we were lucky. On that first night, I sat upstairs in the mezzanine with the other more experienced waitresses and listened to their easy chatter. I tried to eat, but my stomach would not calm down. I was no longer the submarine girl, the counter girl or small time waitress at Howard Johnsons; this was the big time starting tonight. I was scared to death and tried not to show it.

Before people started to arrive, I took a minute to look out from the upstairs mezzanine balcony and examine my surroundings from a different angle. It honestly was like stepping into another world. Floor to ceiling glass windows framed the track and the impressive landscaped green lawn, colorful flower beds and sparkling lake right in the center. A brightly lit scoreboard reflected colors in the water. Sleek, noble trotter horses harnessed to carts driven by jockeys wheeled gracefully around the track. It seemed surreal. This splendor was hidden from view when you approached the building from the front parking lot. Here on the back side of the building was a glamorous playground for the wealthy and big-time gamblers.

Waitress stations consisted of three to five larger tables or eight to ten smaller two-top tables. Stations were assigned by the maître de', Tony, an Italian man with thinning hair who stood about five feet four inches and wore a black, well cut tuxedo. Even though he was short, he looked much taller and oozed pomposity; you could pick him out in any crowd. He would walk ahead of a customer with his palm turned outward down by his side to receive his tip for seating the customer in a prime location. If a customer insulted him by giving him change, not bills, he would drop it on the floor as he walked and I'm sure that customer was seated behind a pole. As it was with customers, the best stations were assigned according to whoever was in Tony's favor on that particular night. Usually this was Betty or one of her friends, like Sylvia. I was dazzled by the formal, showy dining room where a real maître de' greeted and seated people, a real chef worked in the kitchen, and busboys helped carry trays and clean the tables. This was a world I had never known before.

I stood stiffly next to my station down by the windows. This waiting time before customers arrived was both relaxing and nerve-racking. That sounds like an oxymoron, but looking out at the track and lake was tranquil, while waiting for the customers to arrive was not. The club house was arranged on five levels of seating for everyone to get a prime view of the races. If you worked on the lower level, level A, like I did the first night, you constantly ran up and down the five levels of steps for food and drinks, but it was one of the slower paced stations because it had the two-top tables, or seating for two people. The worst part was the distance from the lower station to the bar and kitchen. Thankfully, my first night went smoothly since my section was not very full.

This could not be said for future nights as I ran up and down those levels as fast as my legs would carry me with trays full of drinks and hot food. I dodged around customers who didn't notice me as they were jumping and yelling for their horse to win. It was a good thing our customers had the races to think about as we waited in long lines for cocktails from the bar or food from the kitchen. On busy nights, we fed about 1200 people in a short three-hour period of time. It was chaos and I didn't really embrace chaos.

My first couple of weeks in the clubhouse, I encountered that language barrier lesson again like the lox and bagels at the Riviera Cabana Club. This time it was about drinks. I had never served beer or liquor, so if customers asked for drinks by brand names such as a Cutty Sark or ordered fancy cocktails like a pink lady, grasshopper, daiquiri or sidecar, I was lost. How could I serve a drink if I didn't know what it was or what it looked like? I had to ask Betty for help again, "What in the heck is a Cutty Sark?" I asked. I got the "you are so dense" look as usual, but she helped me out. Cutty Sark was top shelf scotch, which I later found out was one of Betty's favorite drinks. The bartender was always helpful and told me the names of drinks as he placed them on my tray. I watched and remembered. Then there was the colorful language of racing. What is a daily double or daily triple? What did they mean by playing the odds, or place, show and dead heat? My little world of kids and diapers was expanding at a fast pace.

Working at the race track, I learned the fine art of balancing food and drinks on trays as I weaved between customers who did not pay any attention to me or my personal space. After many nights of fear and trembling muscles, I was finally able to carry a large, oval aluminum tray balanced precariously on my shoulder. Some waitresses, waiters, or bus boys were strong enough to carry a tray up high, perched on one hand. Not me. I did not have the strength in my arms, so the tray rested on my shoulder for balance. I found out the hard way that my hand had to be positioned right under the heaviest part of the tray. If the tray was off balance, look out below! It was also difficult to set the heavy tray down on the wobbly tray stand next to the table. The dinners were covered with metal lids with a small, finger sized hole right in the middle of the lid for easy lifting. The lid allowed plates to be stacked two to three high with six to eight on a tray . . . sometimes more for the busboys. I arranged the dinners on the tray in the same order that they were written on my order pad. Writing everything down was a well-learned lesson from my carhop days.

Waitresses carried a smaller tray with a cork bottom to serve drinks so they could not slide around and spill. The veteran waitresses had their own special drink trays, the newer ones, with their names etched into them. They even had hiding places for their special drink trays. If I wanted to keep my head, I learned to take whichever drink tray happened to be left, usually an old worn out one. Sometimes Betty would help me find a better tray to use. If one of the girls happened to be off that night she would show me their hiding spot. I had to promise to put it back at the end of the night. These club house waitresses were a tough crowd and Betty fit right in. I was not really a good fit as a clubhouse waitress, but I managed to make it through most nights unscathed since I was under the Betty protection service.

G.H. Ashenfelter

One memorable incident almost ended my racetrack career early. I cringe when I think about the night our chef Sam slammed a big knife right down inches in front of my face because I forgot and ordered seafood chowder, a dish he said they were out of. It scared me so badly I jumped back and immediately burst into tears. Upset and shaking, I felt about ready to throw up. I took a deep breath to gain control and went back to the customers to explain the dilemma. They could tell I was upset, were sympathetic and changed their order. When I went back to the kitchen with the new order, Sam had special made the original order of seafood chowder for me. He probably felt sorry about scaring me. Did Betty yell at him I wondered? Some of the waitresses were sympathetic, but basically they just felt this was part of my trial by fire or knife, or whatever you wanted to call it.

One time I dropped a whole tray of prime rib dinners down the back steps, luckily out of sight from customers. They were picked up, taken back to the kitchen, washed off, warmed up and reserved with new au jus on clean plates. You can't just throw away expensive prime rib. I won't go into detail about the beer bottle that jumped off my tray and bounced down the mezzanine carpeted steps barely missing a customer. I watched with horror as the foam spewed out of the bottle top all the way down the steps. This job was tough on my nerves.

Even though the race track was a good paying job, as Betty promised, and I earned about $50 to

$100 a night, my stomach was constantly churning, especially at the beginning of each night as I waited for the customers to be seated. For the remainder of the night, I was on automatic pilot for five hours and never stopped running until it was time to go home at eleven. If I didn't give the customers fast service, they complained immediately to Tony, the maître de, and then, there was the cook with the large knife who still intimidated me. I wasn't sure if the stress was worth it at times. It was more in my nature to sit down and relax with a good book, not run my legs off serving food and drinks for distracted customers.

On the other hand, I had good times at the racetrack. I met lots of interesting people and learned about the world of trotter and pacer horses. The other waitresses were kind to me in many ways, probably because I was Betty's sister. Sometimes on a slow night I stood at my station and gazed out at the track. The horses and carts were splendid as they gracefully paced or trotted around the well-manicured track and lake. Although I was never a gambler, I studied the racing form and learned how to read and understand the odds. Betty and I would pool our money and bet on any horse with the name of Brett or Joe. Joe was our brother's name and Brett was her stepson's name. I finally learned about a daily double where you had to pick the winners of the first two races, and I knew the difference between win, place and show. Not a gambler, I hated to lose money and never won much, but it was fun to place a few bets and try to win.

G.H. Ashenfelter

I began to know my sister on a couple of new levels. She was nicer to me in many ways as we worked together, but she also coerced me into taking drinks up to her locker to hide them there so she could drink them during her break or after work. These drinks were mistakes made by the bartender, and instead of throwing them down the drain, the bartender gave them to me and I took them upstairs and set them inside Betty's locker. I knew we weren't supposed to do this, but I almost always did what Betty requested. All of our family did. No questions asked. She was the boss and liked to drink and that was just the way it was in our family.

I only worked one summer at the race track. My part time position as a clubhouse waitress did not bode well with my husband, Earl. On the weekend nights, I would come home around midnight, tired from running up and down steps with heavy trays of food and drinks and the house would be a total wreck. Whenever Earl had to baby-sit, as he called it, for our little girls Earlene and Amber; he would leave the dirty dishes on the table after dinner and the floor would be littered with toys and food. That will teach me to go to work and leave the family! He was also very jealous and possessive because I had lost weight running up and down steps and of course had my smile back. Our marriage was becoming a bit rocky. Considering this, we decided that it would be best if I stayed home and babysat like a proper housewife did in the '60s. So, it was back to only doing housework and washing diapers with no breaks or relief in sight.

20 Jobs: A Memoir

By the beginning of the next year, I was pregnant again. On Wednesday, December 21st, 1966, our new baby boy was born. I went to the doctor on the 21st and he examined me and told me to go home and enjoy Christmas. On the way home, my water broke and we turned right around a headed for Brentwood hospital. There were no ultrasounds in those days, so we didn't know that our baby was a boy. We were delighted when Earl Henry entered the world at seven pounds and 8 ounces. He was named after his two grandfathers. I remember that my husband, Earl, was extremely happy to have a son and so was I because now maybe I could quit having babies.

My mother, who was divorced from my dad, stayed with the girls while I was in the hospital. When I came home with my new baby boy, she had the house cleaned up, the tree up and the living room decorated for Christmas. It was comforting to have her help. I don't remember if I told her how much I appreciated that, but I hope that I did. A few years later, Mom caught a bad case of the flu and ended up in the hospital. February 13, 1969, one day before Valentine's Day, Mom passed away at the early age of 50, from complications of heart, liver and kidney failure. Possibly this was caused from drinking so much after her divorce, but the exact cause of death was not clear. Sad to say, I never felt close to my mom and today realize that I was never the daughter I should have been. I deeply regret that. At the time I don't think I knew how to be that daughter.

Now there was no time to think about working a job since our little Red Fox house was filling up fast with kids. During the summers and on most weekends, my sister Jane and my brother Joe came to live with us. They liked staying with us as opposed to being with their step-mother and step-brothers. It was a break for me since Jane helped babysit the kids. Earl and Joe bonded and would go fishing and hunting together and often took Little Earl with them. Life had a family rhythm that kept me content and busy.

When my son, Little Earl started Kindergarten, I realized that I was pregnant again. So much for the kids being in school all day! On Sunday, May 28th, 1972, our second son Adam was born. It happened on a Sunday afternoon right during the Memorial Day parade. At that time, I was a Girl Scout leader and our troop was supposed to march in the parade that day. Fortunately, I decided not to go. Adam Michael was born about 2:30 in the afternoon, right during the time of the parade, and he weighed ten pounds and one ounce. I chose his name. Even though he was my largest baby, he was my easiest delivery. I even weighed less after the birth than I did when I got pregnant. With four children, we had outgrown our tiny three bedroom slab home.

Feeling a crunch for space, we started looking for a place in the country and finally found a century old, two story farmhouse in Freedom Township with six bedrooms, two bathrooms and four acres of land with a small barn on the property. It was located about ten miles up the road from our current home, so we put in a bid. This was a time, in the early '70s, when interest rates for buying a home were at an all time high, 10 or 11 percent. In spite of this, we went ahead and took out a 30-year mortgage and moved to the country. I was ecstatic and it didn't bother me that the house was not insulated, needed a new well, and had horsehair in the thick plaster walls. The four bedrooms upstairs were in the process of being remodeled but were not finished.

One plus was that the house had a new hot-water radiator furnace, but we didn't realize that the price of fuel oil was going to sky-rocket and it would become a money pit, but no matter, we loved our new home in the country. Earl and I both worked hard and we did enjoy the country life with our four kids, animals, tractors and gardens. The little farm wasn't perfect but living there was never dull and we almost lived happily ever after.

G.H. Ashenfelter

Job 9 - Celery Picker

Covered with a fine layer of black dirt from my hair to my shoes, I stepped inside the enclosed back porch of our big old farmhouse and peeled off layers of dirty shirts and jeans before daring to step foot into the large kitchen. My back was tired and I couldn't wait to hit the shower. Ever since we had moved out to the country, my days were full with raising kids, growing vegetables, keeping chickens and pigs, and selling produce at a roadside stand in front of our century old farmhouse in Freedom. My three older children, Earlene, Amber, and Earl were in school during the day, and my youngest son, Adam, was in kindergarten half a day. My husband worked crazy swing shifts at the US Wire Steel Mill in Cleveland, while I stayed, happily, at home. But then, I got the crazy idea of picking celery for half a day out at Youngblood's farm in Shalersville. Sometimes I am not the smartest chicken in the coop.

20 Jobs: A Memoir

Keeping up with our large garden and vegetable stand along with the house and kids was plenty of work, but not considered a "real" job since there was no paycheck and no Social Security. Nonetheless, I probably worked physically harder on our little farm than at any other time in my life. Every fall, I preserved our garden vegetables for the winter. I canned a hundred quarts of beans, a hundred quarts of tomatoes, chili sauce, sauerkraut, pickles and relishes. In addition, I froze corn, other vegetables and meat from hogs that we butchered. After we had enough food put up for the winter, I sold the leftover vegetables at our little stand in front of the house and used the money to buy the kids' school clothes each year.

Taking care of a drafty, six bedroom 150 year-old house, four kids plus a husband, I exceeded the hours for a full time job. So what possessed me to become a celery picker? Not sure, but when I heard they needed pickers at Youngblood's muck farm on Infirmary Road in Shalersville Township, I decided to give it a try. Does that sound like something a sane person would choose to do? Not really!

My first day as a celery picker began at 9:00 a.m. after my kids were on the bus and off to school. I drove our old pickup truck down to Infirmary Road and pulled into Youngblood's drive and parked. A small group of pickers were congregated next to the driveway by the big farmhouse. I joined them and stood next to a middle aged black lady, a young girl in her twenties, and a couple of middle-aged men. I wondered if they had any other choices in life rather than being celery pickers. Maybe they were out of a job or needed extra money for their household. Who knows, maybe this was their chance to pick up a few extra dollars, like me. Before September, the celery was harvested by teens. Once they were back in school, the farmers were desperate for help to get the celery crop picked on time. So here we were for whatever reason.

Celery will not grow well in any old dirt. It needs special soil called muck. Muck, known as black soil, is made primarily from drained swampland and is excellent for growing crops like celery, potatoes, onions and carrots. Muck soils are extremely rich in nutrients because of the decayed organic material and these soils present some unique challenges for the farmer. Because of the high organic content, the topsoil can be extremely dry, despite the soil's moisture-holding ability that is excellent for root vegetables. Blowing soil can result in annual soil loss. This soil is very friable, meaning that the dark colored, fine soil sticks to everything, and I mean everything! It sticks to clothes, hair and every pore in your skin.

A tractor and wagon pulled up and we were greeted by an elderly couple. They looked like farmers drawn from an Old Dutch master painting with weathered, tan skin and backs slightly bent by hard work. The woman, Frances, was slight but looked durable and wore old baggy pants, a long sleeved shirt and a bandana that covered most of her gray hair. Her husband Pete was stout and dressed like a typical farmer, bibbed overalls over a long sleeved blue shirt with a plaid hankie sticking out of his pocket. I followed the others as we scrambled up onto the flat-bed wagon. Pete drove the tractor and pulled his picking crew down a small hill on a road leading to the celery fields. The air was damp and fresh on my face as we bounced into the first field that was waiting to be harvested.

We jumped down from the wagon and I was given a pair of thick rubber gloves and a big plastic bag to use as an apron to keep my clothes dry. At this time of the morning, the celery leaves were soaked with dew. I slipped the bag over my head, tied some twine around the waist and donned the bulky gloves. Then, I looked at the knives lined up on the wagon and chose the biggest one with the longest blade. If I remember right, the knife was about two feet long, but that may be an exaggeration of memory. I'm not sure why, but it was to become one of the best parts of being a celery picker, wielding my long knife. All ready, I thought, as I picked up my knife and turned to face the long, green row in front of me.

Frances showed me how to harvest the celery stalks that stood tall in the rows, practically up to my waist. That was a surprise. First I grabbed hold of the wet plant with my left hand, bent it sideways and used my right hand to push the point of the knife into the thick celery base next to the ground. I exerted pressure on the knife and snapped the stalk off clean. Well, after more practice, I snapped it off clean.

G.H. Ashenfelter

When the stalks were picked, we stacked them into small wooden crates that sat between the rows. Each crate held about 20 celery stalks and when they were filled, Pete or Frances came along with a huge machete knife and whacked off the top leaves. Now it resembled the celery you see in a store.

I tried to move fast and at least keep up with the other pickers. Although some were older than me, they worked faster and seemed more experienced at picking. They didn't talk much as they worked at a steady rhythm, backs facing the sun. I picked many of the vegetables in our one acre garden, so felt I could do this job with ease. The difference was at home I wasn't required to maintain a steady pace for hours. I worked at my own speed and rested often. Here, the workers moved fast and steady. I wanted to prove I could work as hard as everyone else, so I pushed to keep up the pace.

After steadily picking for two hours, we had a break. Thank goodness because I was beat! I stretched my back before I climbed up to sit on the edge of the flatbed wagon. Gratefully, I drank my coffee and ate the snack that Frances brought for the pickers. She handed us only one little snack cake even though I could have eaten the whole box. Nobody asked for seconds, so I didn't either. I learned later that it was a well known fact that Frances was frugal and we only got one snack each.

Looking back to that first day, I can picture me dressed like a hobo in a plastic bag, covered in dirt, sitting on a flatbed wagon surrounded by fields of bright green celery and black muck, eating a Ho Ho. It was completely opposite from the fancy race track with the starched, white linen tablecloths and shiny water goblets. But I didn't miss the hustle and bustle of hundreds of people drinking, eating and gambling. Here in the muck, where the earth moved under your feet whenever the tractor drove by, I felt more comfortable and at peace, but tired.

Working in an open field, wielding a knife to chop down celery connected me to a long ago tradition of hunters and gatherers, or even to the more modern tradition of migrant workers who worked long hours in the sun - instead of a measly four hours like I did. Outside, so close to nature, I could smell the damp celery and taste the gritty dirt on my tongue. On crisp fall mornings, the bright celery leaves glistened with dew, the sun caressed my face and I could even go so far as to say I enjoyed it. Nonetheless, it was back breaking work.

Later after the leaves dried, I peeled off the garbage bag. Under it I wore a long-sleeved man's shirt and jeans and there was a precise reason for this attire. If bare arms were exposed, pickers could easily catch something called celery poisoning from the wet celery leaves. Nobody mentioned this to me at first. Unfortunately, soon after I started picking, I did catch it. Bumps broke out all over my arms and chest and it looked and itched just like poison ivy. In spite of this discomfort, I continued to show up and pick celery, covered with calamine lotion under my shirt.

G.H. Ashenfelter

Because we cut the stalk off close to the ground, the dirt quickly dulled the blades of the knives. When the stalks didn't snap off as easily for me, it was time to get my knife sharpened. Pete sharpened the knives for us, and he took great pride in this process as he expertly swished the knife blade back and forth over the dark whetstone. This gave me a chance to stand up straight, stretch my back and chat with Pete. I liked his calm deep voice that held the hint of a Dutch accent. When we talked, I found out that their family was from the Netherlands and their grown children were not interested in running the celery farm. He seemed sad about that, but I was not surprised since the farm required intensive labor for a celery crop. Pete was more amiable than Frances and took his time with the sharpening, maybe so we could visit longer.

The little wooden crates full of celery sat between the flattened picked rows and then Pete came along in a small front end loader to lift the crates and load them into huge square boxes. When the big boxes were full, he loaded them onto the flat bed wagon. At the end of the day, we climbed back on the wagon and sat next to these big square crates as we rode back up to the barn.

One day a large truck was waiting in the driveway to pick up the celery. It said "Campbell's" on the side in big red letters. I was awe-struck to learn that the celery I picked was sold to Campbell's Soup Company. Most families in my generation ate Campbell's Soup for lunch and used it as a main ingredient in dinner casseroles. After learning this new tidbit, every time we had soup at home, I would say to the kids that maybe the celery in the soup was picked by their mom. Sorry to say, they were not that impressed. Probably because most of the food they ate was picked by their mom anyhow.

I picked celery in the fall for maybe two or three years from the beginning of September to the end of October. Sometimes I took our youngest son Adam with me if he was off school. He played happily in the black muck while I chopped down the stalks of celery. We were both covered with dirt when we got home. I can't remember how much they paid workers, maybe four or five dollars an hour, but I do remember that in the corner of my paycheck was an image of a little stalk of celery that clearly showed how this money was earned.

One bright fall morning when I was driving our old Ford truck to the celery farm, I drove right by the dirt driveway and decided that I didn't want to work in the muck that day. I felt a twinge of guilt, but ignored it, turned around and headed back home. It was easy to justify this action at the time. It was common for the other workers to not show up to pick every day. I further rationalized that the pay check was a mere pittance for all my hard work and it didn't really help us out that much. I had plenty of other work to do around our own little farm. I was full of lame excuses.

G.H. Ashenfelter

After that day, I never went back to picking celery, and I'm ashamed to admit that I didn't even call or tell the sweet old couple why I never returned to the celery fields. I wasn't exactly sure and couldn't explain it even to myself. I wasn't a lazy person, but I didn't want to pick celery anymore. How I wish that I had been honest and faced them to tell them I quit instead of just not showing up for work.

Pete and Frances have both passed on and the celery fields lay empty. I think their son sells real estate. For sure, celery is a difficult crop to grow and harvest. Nobody in their family wanted to continue on with this hard working life. In my mind's eye, I can picture their weathered faces and remember their kind eyes - Frances in her bandana handing us our snack and Pete carefully sharpening my knife. Sometimes I feel the earth move under me like a tractor and wagon just rumbled by with a load of celery crates. Yes, even years later, I feel regret that I left with no explanation. They both deserved better than that.

Breakup

How easy it is to break a marriage
Crack the shell and let it seep
Crush it with a giant footstep
Taken right before the leap

How easily can the vows be broken
Shattered in a splintered heap
Smash them hard upon a doorstep
Crossed one night forever deep

How hard to put it back together
Glue will never mend the shards
Everything was tossed asunder
It's time to send you "best regards"

Job 10 - Howard Johnson's Turnpike

If this was a memoir about my marriage or love life, which it's not, I'd say that in that respect my life seemed ill-fated. This was especially true in 1980 when my marriage fell apart. It would take another whole book to try to explain what happened. In retrospect, to be fair, it was not entirely his fault and not all mine either. Many blamed my husband Earl at that time. Unfortunately, I let them. It was easier to play the victim. The common belief of friends and family was that he was the cause of our breakup since he had a girlfriend. In my heart of hearts though, I knew that I was the one throwing our marriage away. The fact that he found another woman did not surprise me. It takes two people working together to make a marriage and we were no longer doing that. I knew what he expected from me; I just couldn't give it anymore.

We both hurt each other and unfortunately, we also hurt our four children. After years of looking back and wondering why, I can only sum it up by saying that I wanted something else, maybe my freedom or an imaginary romance. It's hard to define why we were no longer happy together. I know that by saying "He wanted his freedom, or I wanted my freedom" is a cliché, one used by many people to end a marriage, but there is no easy way to answer to our actions.

Earl left the house, and I got my freedom, all right. Along with the freedom came the four acre farm, the bills, the dogs, the cats, the chickens, and the four kids. To sum it up in the words of a sad country song, "You picked a fine time to leave me . . . with four hungry kids and a crop in the field." It was all left up to me and I wasn't prepared to handle it.

In the early '80s, there was also a recession that had a great impact on the price of fuel oil and gasoline. In winter we heated our six bedroom century home with fuel oil, but when the price went sky high, we could not afford to buy it. We had installed a wood burner to save money on heating fuel, but our wood pile was low and the man of the house who cut the wood was gone. The kids and I tried to cut and stack wood, but it was impossible to keep up with heating that huge house. I remember driving to Ravenna and begging the people in the fuel oil company to give us oil on credit. The men in the office hardly looked at me and showed no signs of pity. They turned me down flat and advised me to apply for welfare. It stung when they told me that. I had never applied for any kind of welfare and didn't even know where to start. Maybe it was my pride, but that quickly left town along with my husband. Yes, I was free, but on the verge of losing our house and desperate for money to feed the kids and pay the bills.

G.H. Ashenfelter

I did what I knew how to do best; I looked for a job. Out in Freedom Township, the nearest employment opportunity was across the field from our house, Howard Johnson's. At that time, it was the only restaurant where a traveler could stop and eat on the Ohio Turnpike. My kids used to walk straight across the field from our house, go in the open back gate and buy candy or snacks. Also, my two teenage daughters, Amber and Earlene, had previously worked at the turnpike plaza. Howard Johnson's was less than a mile away, which was a plus since my old truck was not only rusty, but not too trusty.

My life had turned on its heel, so applying for a job on the turnpike seemed like my best choice at the time. I filled out the application, and with my background in waitress work, I easily got the job. It didn't pay much, but I had not worked outside the home in many years and didn't have many choices. This was my best option, so here I was, back at good old Ho Jo's. Isn't life ironic!

My new waitress job was nothing like my previous job at the Warrensville Heights Howard Johnson's. Howard Johnson's on the Ohio Turnpike was not a restaurant style place where you wait on customers while someone else cooks the food. No, not at all! It was a line job where a server did the whole enchilada: cook, clean, stock and serve.

On my first day, I was working the morning shift to replace Pearl, a woman who was on sick leave. My job was to make toast and cook eggs to order behind a Plexiglas window on a little grill that was visible to customers as they walked down the line. At home, I was a competent cook and had made dozens of eggs for my family. After all, we did raise chickens. How hard can this be? That first morning, the customers were trickling down the line picking up their juice, coffee and fruit dishes. When they got to me, I smiled my biggest good morning smile and prepared their eggs and toast. The scrambled eggs were easy since they were pre-mixed in a carton and ready to pour, but the other eggs had to be cooked to order. At the beginning, I was cooking one or two eggs at a time with no problems. This isn't difficult, I thought.

Then I looked up and saw that the line was packed with people clear out to the door. It was a bus load of people! My heart rate picked up as my hands started to move faster and shake with anxiety. As the bus people moved down the line, it seemed that they all wanted eggs cooked in every imaginable way; sunny side up, over easy, one minute, three minutes and no runny whites. They impatiently peered over and through the clear partition as they watched me break their eggs onto the overflowing grill surface.

I suddenly became so nervous that I couldn't cook a decent egg. My face grew hotter than the grill as eggs started slipping from my hands and breaking everywhere. They stuck to the evil grill and some even fell on the floor and landed on my once-white shoes. It was an egg nightmare straight out of a Dr. Seuss book:

"How do you want your eggs, Madam?
At this point, I don't give a damn!"

G.H. Ashenfelter

The impatient bus people were not happy about their messed up egg orders, although some were more understanding. At this point my happy smile was gone, my head hurt and I could not even look up into the faces to determine if the customers were angry or sympathetic. They were in a hurry to get back on the bus and the bumbling line server couldn't cook a decent egg. I was a nervous wreck. Finally, after what seemed like hours, the line of people ended. I made it through the breakfast fiasco. I stepped back, blinked, swallowed down the big lump in my throat and looked down at the mess on the floor and my yellow, yolky shoes. I took a deep breath. I was not going to cry or give up.

After that trial by fire, I found out a little secret; the grill had to be at an exact temperature so eggs wouldn't stick. Obviously, I didn't know that on the first day. Soon I became more efficient as a line cook, but I knew that this was not a job that I wanted to keep doing forever.

Pearl came back to work on day shift and in spite of her reputation of being stern, it turned out that she had a kind heart. She was very serious about her work, like Little Bit was at Kresge's. She was always neat as a pin plus courteous and sincere, a real lady. I admired her work ethics and we soon became friends. She was maybe 10 years older than me with dark hair and complexion; her soft, dark eyes seemed to see right through a person. At work, I didn't talk about my impending divorce, but once I broke down and confided in Pearl. Her eyes filled with pity as she put her arms around me and said, "Oh, you poor thing." That hug almost did me in. I was pitiful alright, but I couldn't let emotions creep into my workplace or I would break down. After that, I was careful not to tell anyone else. I couldn't talk about how my life was falling apart and certainly didn't want to try to explain it to anyone since I didn't understand it myself.

A few months later, I decided to apply as the night shift supervisor, although I hated to leave day shift and would miss seeing Pearl. Working nights, I could sleep when the kids were in school, be home to make supper, and then go to work while they slept. My oldest daughter Earlene was 17, her sister Amber was 16. My son, Earl was 14 and my youngest son Adam was 8. I felt that I could leave them alone at night, but I didn't really like it. It eased my guilt to know that I was five minutes away and we had a big German Shepherd dog named Joe who would not let a stranger in the house. At the time, there seemed like no other choice. After the kids were in bed, I would jump in the old truck and drive the mile to Howard Johnson's to work the night shift.

Night supervisor meant that I was in charge of me along with one other person. We stocked shelves, prepared food lines, waited on customers, cleaned the bathrooms, and frosted the donuts. This kept me constantly in motion and the nights went by in a tired blur. Most of the late night customers were truck drivers, so night shift was perfect for my newly separated situation. Their attention and friendly conversation was a salve to my wounded ego.

In the midnight hours, I swallowed down my sadness along with the frosted donuts that I often brought home to the kids for breakfast. One would think this was a fattening job with all the donuts, but not on the divorce diet; most of the time I couldn't eat much of anything and ended up losing about 25 pounds.

Working night shift at Howard Johnson's was lonely and confusing as I stood in the kitchen spreading frosting on donut after donut, trying not to think sad thoughts. It was difficult to sleep days. I was bone tired. I cried myself to sleep every night, or morning, not only for my broken marriage, but for the loss of my life as I had known it for the past 18 years. Nothing felt normal. Probably it was a perfect time in my life to see a psychiatrist or get counseling, but it didn't seem like a viable option for me. My sisters and dad were trying to be supportive, but I was ashamed of myself and my broken marriage. I couldn't ask for their help.

At work I always kept up a good front, but my stomach hurt constantly. The pain was real, like I had been kicked in the gut. In hindsight, working probably saved me from a nervous breakdown. I had to pull myself together each night to make the donuts, clean the restrooms and stock up the shelves for morning. I put on my happy mask and didn't allow myself to fall apart.

Barely functioning on night shift and not making much money, only enough to buy food, but not enough to pay our bills, I knew this had to end. I stopped opening any envelopes if they looked like a bill and threw them all in a heap. Our fractured family had serious financial problems and we were in danger of losing everything. My husband had left his job at US Steel so we no longer had health insurance. He also opted not to send me any support money for the kids.

I decided to search for more gainful employment and started looking in Twinsburg, which was a half hour drive from Freedom and hosted a large industrial parkway. It was clear that I had to get some kind of health insurance for us. The best place would be in a factory, mainly because factories offered medical benefits and paid better money than Howard Johnson's.

I began searching for work, door to door, factory to factory. After a couple of weeks of visiting each identical, square, brick building and filling out numerous applications, I finally landed my first manufacturing job at an electronics factory in Twinsburg. They must have been desperate for help since they hired me with no prior factory experience and for this I was grateful. It was time to begin a new job and a new chapter in my life.

G.H. Ashenfelter

Job 11 – Western Reserve Electronics

Driving down Interstate 480 in my rusty, green Ford pickup truck, I adjusted the blanket around my knees to keep my legs warm. The heater was on, but wind blew directly in through the hole on the passenger side where the floor was rusted clear through. I could see the road in front of me and below me. Lucky there are no holes on the driver's side, I thought to myself. I was on the way to my new factory job at Western Reserve Electronics, a small electronics plant located by Crown Hill Cemetery in Twinsburg.

My life was off balance due to the recent separation from my husband and the devastating loss of income and security. Starting a new line of work was daunting since I didn't know what to expect in a factory or what was expected of me. Until this day, I had only served and prepared food or picked celery crops. I knew how to handle hard work and how to serve customers but never worked in manufacturing before.

I arrived and parked my truck in the back of the bumpy, gravel parking lot. Next to me sat older model cars and trucks, rusted and dented, so my truck fit right in. I ground the floor gear shift into reverse so the truck wouldn't roll, and jumped out. I pulled down my T-shirt, zipped up my jacket and entered the side door of the long building.

Inside, women of various ages sat and chatted at tables in the front area of a large open room. There were a few men among them. I stood by quietly, not sure what to do, taking it all in, until a bell rang. Then everyone, except me, got up and moved to one of the long production tables situated around the open room. I stood there feeling lost until I was approached by a woman about my age who introduced herself as Thelma, my trainer and mentor. We walked together to some unoccupied chairs at a long table that was cluttered with an assortment of unfamiliar hand tools. Around the tables, women sat, their heads bowed intently as they fiddled with some kind of small green boards. Fluorescent light fixtures hung close overhead and provided bright, direct lighting above the tables. A smell of something hot like burning metal mixed with background music and the light chatter of voices. It was nothing like I had ever experienced before. I tried to calm my churning stomach. I chewed my lower lip and smiled weakly at Thelma. She returned my half smile to reassure me that it would be fine. I wasn't so sure.

Thelma was a little older than me with curly, short brown hair and a pleasant face. She was calm and did not act like any boss I had ever known before. We both put on white cotton gloves. Then she picked up the funny green board and patiently demonstrated how to use a small hot iron to melt the silver solder on the back of the green board, which I later learned was called a PC board. She showed me how to use a little tube with a plunger to suck the melted metal, which looked like mercury, out of the holes. As the solder melted, Thelma placed the tip of the tube over the silver glob and pushed down on the plunger. When released, the plunger sprang back up, whoosh, the slippery solder disappeared out of the hole just like magic. This little tool was called a solder sucker and the name fit perfectly.

When I clumsily tried to copy Thelma's actions, it didn't go very well, but there was no pressure at this new job, so I just kept practicing on junk boards. After awhile, I got the hang of it and was leaving little empty holes all over the boards. Not so bad, I thought, even kind of fun! The morning passed by in a flash of melted, sucked-up silver solder and before I knew it, it was lunch time. The afternoon passed quickly and soon the day was over. Concentrating on fixing these PC boards took my mind off my problems. I just had to follow Thelma's instructions, look for mistakes on the boards and fix them.

I learned more and more about PC boards each passing day. The solder on the PC boards formed a connection between the assorted diodes, resistors and transistors. Some looked like little striped doodle bugs with legs. The solder connection on these legs was important in order for the board to function. If there was a hole in the solder or a bridge between two holes, the PC board wouldn't work right. For the bridged solder, it was an easy fix, melt it with the hot iron and get rid of the bridge. This was less complicated than sucking out the solder. It took some time to get the hang of fixing PC boards, but nobody seemed to care about speed like they did in a restaurant. No customers were watching and waiting for food and drinks to be served, or eggs to be cooked just right. Factory work was not so bad, I thought.

Working at Western Reserve reminded me of the times when I used to go to ceramic classes with my sister-in-law Michelle. In ceramic class, we would sit and talk while we got lost in painting a tree branch or sanding off a rough spot on a ceramic figurine. It was calming to do ceramics as we chatted between brush strokes. It felt similar as I sat and worked on these boards and chatted with my co-workers. I needed some peace and order in my life at this time. Eventually I became proficient at fixing and repairing PC boards and learned that these boards were used in computers and electronics.

I took pride in my job of fixing these boards and settled right in to this new factory work environment. The days flew by, and then the weeks and months. Eventually I took a test and became a certified solderer, complete with a certificate, my first certificate ever. I caught on to factory work faster than I thought I would.

Although I liked the work, there were some drawbacks of working at Western Reserve Electronics. The pay was not great, maybe seven or eight dollars an hour, but with hospitalization benefits. Besides the low pay, there was our crazy foreman Ray, who would throw a fit like a two year old brat for any given reason. For instance, if you parked in the dock loading zone, even by mistake, you were in big trouble. One morning, madman Ray ran out screaming at a new girl who accidently parked in the loading zone and he fired her on the spot.

I was shocked to witness this extreme childish behavior from a foreman. One recently hired co-worker, Pat, quit her job in protest when this happened. She was a spunky girl newly laid off from General Electric and was used to a different work environment, one that was sensible and fair. I admired her morals, but was not in the position to do the same thing. After that, I made double sure that I parked in the right place each morning. I needed this job, low pay, ranting foreman and all, because it gave me health insurance and it was also a day job with weekends off. Unfortunately, I still wasn't making enough money.

To meet my bills, I acquired a part time job working Friday and Saturday nights back at - guess where - good old Northfield Racetrack. Not my favorite job, but I still did it. I worked with my sister, Betty and her daughter Linda. Betty was still a waitress in the clubhouse and now her daughter worked in the kitchen as a salad girl. Betty had secured jobs at the race track for not only Linda, but her other daughters, Carla, Nadine and step-son Brett. In addition, my sister Jane had worked there as a salad girl and my brother Joe as a bus boy. All thanks to Betty. We were like the Northfield Race Track dynasty clan. In spite of being with my dear sister and niece, I did not look forward to the weekends.

The fast pace of the track was still nerve-racking, plus I was usually bone tired from getting up early and working five days a week in the factory. I dreaded the hectic pace of waiting on the demanding customers and preferred the laid back atmosphere at the factory. Still for the money, I worked two jobs for three years, weekdays at Western Reserve and Friday and Saturday nights at the racetrack.

In spite of low pay and Ranting Ray, working at Western Reserve Electronics helped get me through a difficult time in my life. The radio usually played light rock music in the background and I liked my co-workers. Our hands kept moving and the day did too as we talked or sang along to the radio. One girl I especially enjoyed sitting next to was Nina. She had a great voice and I loved to hear her sing. She was plain looking, had a bad complexion and wore no makeup to hide it. She had long, straight black hair and maybe was part American Indian. Later I found out that she sang part time with a rock band, well no wonder she sang so well with the radio. Her brother Ed worked with us in the shop. He was a machinist and ran the big solder machine where the stuffed PC boards floated across a river of flowing solder.

Ed was a real character, always making us laugh about something or another. He was tall, so tall that when we lined up to leave at the end of the work day he would sometimes get down on his knees to talk face to face to a short, sweet older lady, Essie.

She laughed and giggled like a school girl. He made her day complete. I liked the people at this shop. I was making new friends and finally starting to smile more - my stomach didn't hurt as much either.

Another co-worker I liked working next to was Bott, not sure if that was her real name, but that is what we called her. Sometimes when we worked on the boards and ran out of conversation, she would throw out questions for us to think about. For instance - what was the worst or best thing that ever happened to you? If you could travel anywhere, where would you go? Or what would you do with a million dollars? Discuss! And we did. I liked to think about questions like that. It took my mind off my problems, especially since I was not sure where my life was headed. Separated from my husband, I didn't really know who I was anymore and had never thought about these questions before while busy raising my four kids. Anything that distracted me from my present situation was welcome.

Working at Western Reserve, I had opportunities to discover and develop new skills. I learned to assemble mainframes for the "fisch finders." Before the new age of personal computers, these large machines were used to store and retrieve information. In fact, they are still around today to use for reading microfilm. To assemble these mainframes I used power screwdrivers and other assorted tools. It was a challenge, and at first I was clumsy with these bizarre guy tools, but my skills improved. I learned to ask for help, especially from my mentor Thelma.

20 Jobs: A Memoir

If I couldn't make a part fit, we would figure it out together. When I finally assembled my first main frame and the parts fit together properly, it was like giving birth to a robot. I was the proud mama. Using power tools was empowering. No wonder guys liked them.

Just when I had this mechanical assembly job down to a science and could very easily assemble the main frames, the factory shifted gears. The fische-finder job was put on hold and Western Reserve workers took on the formidable task of constructing cables for the M1 Battle Tanks. This was before the time of Desert Storm and we were not yet aware of why there would be great demand for these tank cables, but suddenly they became our main focus. Never a dull moment at Western Reserve Electronics! The foreman and engineer stressed that this was an important contract and we had new skills to learn and master.

After the PC boards and mechanical assembly, I could tackle anything. My willingness to plunge into new projects must have made an impression on the foreman or engineer because I was promoted to a line leader with nine girls working under me. My team was assigned to build one of the biggest tank cables. The title of "Line Leader" gave me a boost in status and responsibility, but no boost in pay. One thing worked out well for me - I discovered that I had the ability to work well with others in a leadership role. I never knew I had that knack, but it emerged.

G.H. Ashenfelter

The girls on my team liked me and worked hard to please me. I tried to be upbeat, fair, and hard-working. I assigned the jobs on the cable to fit the individual skills of each girl and we worked well together. It was gratifying to be in charge of a team and to solve problems. I liked the challenge and looked forward to going to work each day.

It might be dull to describe the exact details of how to build a cable, but I can't resist giving a quick overview of the process. First we measured and cut the wires to a specified length. There were about 30 or 40 wires of assorted colors in our cable. We laid them out in a predetermined pattern on a standing board that was about six feet long. Try to picture a long bunch of assorted colored wires that branch out like tree branches to different endings. After the wires were put in place, they were banded together with plastic ties to form a solid mass that could then be lifted from the board.

The most difficult part of the cable was covering the bundled wires with rubber tubes - sort of like putting a rubber skin on a snake or tugging up tight pantyhose. It took a couple of girls to pull the rubber tubing in place. After the tubing was on, the cable was placed on a heat bed, which shrank the rubber tubing down and held the wires tightly together. Color coded wires were left sticking out the ends. Then a worker plugged the wires into matching color metal connectors. This took nimble fingers and one girl on my team was an expert at that, Jen. I tried to assign jobs to fit each girl, if possible.

111

My cable team had one complaint about me as their fearless leader. I would too often lend out our tools to other teams. I thought it was nice to share. But it backfired because whenever we needed a certain tool, my girls would have to go and search for it. After awhile, they started hiding tools from me so I wouldn't lend them out. Other than that, we got along fine.

One girl on my cable team, Connie, who was laid off from General Electric Lamp Plant in Ravenna, had a lasting impact on my life. Connie was a little younger than me, always wore a curly perm in her dark hair and loved to talk. We became close friends and she often told me that I should apply for a job at General Electric when they started hiring again because I would fit right in, plus they paid so much more than Western Reserve Electronics.

This idea of "more pay" appealed to me, so when Connie got called back to GE, I followed her advice on how I could get hired in. First off, I had to be registered with the unemployment office in Ravenna. At that time, GE only hired through that office. Connie told me to keep bugging them to send me for an interview. I repeatedly registered at the office and followed up each week with a phone call. Finally, my persistence worked. Six months after Connie was called back to work, General Electric Lamp Plant called me for an interview.

Even though I enjoyed my work for the three years at Western Reserve Electronics, it hardly paid my bills, even with the part time employment at Northfield Racetrack. During those years, my daughters moved out and started their own lives. Earlene, my oldest daughter, left home to attend Kent State. She later dropped out but then went on to Bohecker College and earned a business degree. After that, to my dismay, she met a man and moved to Pittsburgh where she found a job in human resources. Amber, my younger daughter, also met a man and eventually married him. She worked at East Park Restaurant and was soon expecting.

In April, 1983, the day I turned 40, Amber became a mom and I became a grandmother to a lovely little girl named April who was a joy with her sweet disposition, dark shiny hair and big bright eyes. In January of 1985, Amber delivered Melissa, my second little granddaughter. She looked totally opposite from April, but still lovely with sky blue eyes, blonde hair and healthy lungs. She looked more like her mom. I was excited to be the grandmother of two sweet little girls. Many weekends, April and Melissa stayed with me when Amber had to work - I delighted in my time that I spent with them.

Eventually, I had to file bankruptcy and lost my century old farm house in the country. I was not getting any child support even though it was part of our separation agreement. It seemed that the courts had a hard time enforcing child support in the '80s. My two sons, Earl and Adam, moved with me to a small basement apartment on Lake Street in Kent. We were officially moved out from the country and that made me sad. I had to accept the fact that our family was changing. Now we had to adjust to our new lives.

I was thankful for my years at Western Reserve. This factory job and my new, single friends helped me transition from married life to single life. I developed the confidence to be a line leader and to try my hand at new projects. As I soldered and built cables, I slowly evolved from being a couple to being an individual person. It was painful. I lost touch with most of my married friends. It seemed like I separated from them as well as my husband. Now I had a different life with new single friends. My divorce was finalized during the time I worked at Western Reserve.

∞∞∞∞∞∞∞∞∞

The day of my divorce hearing, I remember sitting alone in an empty waiting room at the Ravenna Court House waiting to see the judge. It was quiet, so quiet that when I heard footsteps coming down the hall, immediately I realized they were my ex-husband's footsteps. They were as familiar as the beat of an old, favorite song. He came around the corner, dressed in a suit instead of his usual jeans and t-shirt. He avoided looking directly at me and his face was aloof and distant like a stranger's. He didn't even speak to me. I turned my head away and pretended indifference, but was suddenly overcome with a deep sadness - for better or worse, I knew my life would never be the same. How can you be married for 18 years and not care about or even acknowledge your spouse? Now I saw my marriage like a favorite dress that had once fit me perfectly well, but had become too tight and was out of style; plus I couldn't get the stains out. I didn't want to throw it away, but I couldn't wear it anymore. We were granted the divorce.

Rites of Divorce

None gather together
To separate two
Who failing each other
Must now start anew

A white silk beginning
An ending abrupt
Bankrupt of feeling
Joy seems corrupt

With this ring no more wed
Love, honor, obey
Will now be unsaid
As vows roll away

Do you take this man
Till death do you part?
Do you take this woman
The one with no heart?

G.H. Ashenfelter

Job 12 – General Electric - Part 1

The parking lot at General Electric was paved velvet smooth, not full of pot holes like the lot at Western Reserve. I glided in and hid my old rusty car behind two newer and bigger cars. Then I approached the gleaming glass office door and tried to look confident, while barely breathing. I did not want to jinx this interview. Armed with three years of factory experience at Western Reserve Electronics and my new found assurance as a line leader, I was ready to wow them at the elusive General Electric, the place where I had tried for six months to get an interview. When I entered, a secretary greeted me and guided me across the thick carpet and into a clean air conditioned office space. I sat down, took a deep breath and curled my hands under on my lap to hide my half chewed nails.

     The Human Resource woman approached with a smile. She was tall and blonde with every hair in place and dressed like a personal shopper from Macy's. She introduced herself as Sandy and led me into a small side office for the interview. I sat down and leaned forward in my leather backed chair as we shared polite conversation. Sandy asked if I knew anyone who currently worked at the GE plant. I told her about my friend Connie and how we worked together at Western Reserve Electronics. She seemed pleased with that tidbit of information. Maybe knowing someone on the inside helped even more than the unemployment bureau. I hoped that was the case. After a few more questions about my work experience, she said they would call me about the open position. I thanked her and left, feeling optimistic. All I had to do now was wait for a phone call.

It seemed like an eternity, but it was only a few days later as I sat drinking my afternoon coffee, when the phone rang. I practically dropped the mug as my heart jumped in my chest. I grabbed up the receiver and took a deep breath. "Hello," I answered nervously. A formal voice confirmed my gut feeling. It was General Electric! Halleluiah and amen! I had gotten the job and could start work the following week on second shift. To say that I was excited would be an understatement. I was ecstatic and started jumping up and down on the basement apartment floor like a kid on a new trampoline as dollar signs danced in my head. I was going to work at GE, the dream job for factory workers in this area. They stressed that I'd be on probation for six weeks, but who cared. They paid well, had great benefits and were often called Generous Electric. For those reasons alone, I would have licked the glass off the factory floor.

G.H. Ashenfelter

Now that working at GE was a reality, I regretted that I would have to leave Western Reserve and my friends. Still I couldn't pass up this chance to make more money, enough money to live on while working only one job. Imagine that! The first thing I planned to do was quit working weekends at the race track, and I did just that - quit the track, said my goodbyes to my cable team at Western Reserve and moved on.

I arrived early for second shift at General Electric in my beat up red car that my dad helped me buy. The old ford pick-up truck with the holes in the floor had fallen apart, and this newer one wasn't far behind. Starting a new job should be a little easier by now, I thought, but tiny birds were flitting around in my stomach trying to poke their way out. I parked toward the back of the lot and made sure that nobody was looking as I crawled out the driver side window. My car doors wouldn't open from the inside. Truly a safety hazard, but in those days if the car ran, it was fine with me. I maneuvered my legs and butt out the window, opened the door from the outside and cranked the window back up. There! All set to go. I straightened my shirt down over my jeans, ran a hand through my hair and headed towards the wide side door.

Once inside, I walked straight over to the big glass display window and looked down at the factory floor. I didn't know it yet, but the GE Lamp Plant was a showcase factory for the company. The big window was there for visitors to see the modern factory at work. As I scrutinized this new place of employment, I saw an acre of ginormous rotating machines spread out before me with a main walkway down the center. The tan tile floors were clean and shiny. Rotating steel machines gleamed brightly as they caught the reflections of large light bulbs circling around open fires. On the high ceiling, color coded blue and orange pipes mingled with vast metal air vents and formed an artful geometric maze.

Huge, bulbous lamps, protruding from tan burlap baskets moved down the lines between the machines. Workers methodically picked them up and loaded them on the next machine. So this was how a factory assembly line looked, I thought. Compared to Western Reserve, which was a free style dance, GE was a well choreographed tango. Everything moved in unison to the clicking rhythm of the machinery.

Exactly at 3:24, a bell rang for first shift to end and the machines stopped. An army of workers, mainly women, flowed out from the factory floor and headed up the stairs. I passed them on my way down, put on my safety glasses and walked through the double doors onto the factory floor for the first time. It was like going from the lunch counter to the race track all over again. This was big time manufacturing - this was General Electric. The machines started back up and constant clattering clicks beat a staccato over the noise of the roaring air vents. No music would be played in here.

Glenn, my new foreman, led me down to my first job on Line 6. Then he introduced me to a man named Vance who would train me on the line. Vance wore faded jeans and a blue button shirt covered with an apron. He looked slightly older than I was and spoke with a southern accent that was calm and reassuring. Glenn left me with Vance. Following his instructions, I put on white cotton gloves and an apron. Then I picked up my first jumbo light bulb that was coming down the line in a burlap basket. It was about ten times larger than a household bulb. I bent a wire down into a dent on the glass bulb and loaded the glass straw, which protruded from where the base would eventually be formed, into a hole on the machine, which I later learned was called the exhaust machine. I turned a handle to close a valve. That was it. The bulb traveled around through the exhaust machine and the air was sucked out through the straw. It came out ready to be sealed, by Vance, who sealed up the glass straw with a little torch. Now it was placed in a basket and sent down the line to the next machine.

It wasn't long before I got the gist of the loading job and kept up with the line pretty easily. I thought to myself, is this all I do? Well no, not really. The exhaust machine could turn snarky if the glass straws broke off in the holes, which happened pretty often. When that happened, I grabbed the air hose and blew the broken glass out the holes causing little pieces of glass to fly everywhere. Yikes – a good thing we wore safety glasses. It was easier if Vance stopped the machine, and he did at first, but he stressed we really didn't want to do that too often -

production was important. First lesson at GE, you have to learn to keep up with the line.

When a week passed of watching lamps roll down the line, loading them on the machine and blowing out glass, the job began to be tedious. I suddenly missed my autonomy and interaction with my team at Western Reserve. Now, I was tied to this line for eight hours.

I kept reminding myself how much money I was making. Vance and I talked a lot, that helped, but the clock was slowing down. Then he asked if I'd like to learn tipping – not with cows, but with a torch. I said, of course I would, especially since that was a sit down job and something new besides bending wires and loading bulbs onto the machine. A tipper carefully melted the glass straw with a tiny torch and formed a glass tip to seal up the bulb. It was a lot more challenging than loading bulbs onto the machine.

The bulbs were extremely hot when they came out of the machine, so I acquired my own pair of cork fingered gloves - all the latest rage at GE. Vance showed me how to glue pieces of cork on the fingers of heavy gloves which then allowed the operator to handle the hot bulbs without burning his or her fingers. With time, practice and patience, I finally learned to be a decent tipper and that broke up the monotony of just loading the bulbs. It was more challenging and time went faster. The exhaust machine was my first of many, many jobs at GE.

G.H. Ashenfelter

Second shift started at 3:24 pm and ended at 11:36 pm. Workers got a 24 minute lunch and two ten minute breaks, perfectly timed by shrill bells, much like the bells at school. My education prepared me for something, following the bells. Connie said that GE was very strict about perfect attendance and being on time. "Don't even be late one time during your probation," she warned. I took her words to heart and was over half an hour early for my first day and every day after. For my six weeks of probation, and years after, I was never late and even worked through a case of the flu that caused me to keep running off the line to throw up. I probably looked awful because the machine adjuster, Joe, who usually said nothing to me, looked sympathetic. He told me that I could go home if necessary.

"Oh, no, no," I protested, "Not while I was on probation." He shook his head and walked away, probably wondering if he was going to catch the flu from me. I stayed on the line, determined to keep this job at any cost.

A month passed by on the exhaust machine, and I was getting tired of Vance's company. Then, in the nick of time, I got a promotion from the line and became an arc tube mounter. Arc tube mounters sat and worked at a table with other women. It was more like the work I was used to doing at Western Reserve. Time went much faster since it was more engaging, and happily, I was with Connie again. She kept me entertained with her constant stream of chatter. I liked working by her.

Our work tables were situated in the back half of the factory away from the loud machinery, so we could talk to each other while our hands moved non-stop welding metal pieces together. Time was speeding up for me.

An arc tube mounter used a spot welder to seal the metal parts together, which formed a frame that held the arc tube in place. The metal parts were arranged in a certain order on the table so they could quickly be picked up and welded in place. The finished arc tube mounts were then loaded into large Multi Vapor light bulbs and sent on to be loaded on the exhaust machine. With a quota to meet, we worked as fast as possible. My forearms became speckled with little burn marks from the sparks that flew out from the welder and landed on my flesh. It didn't hurt, but it left tiny scars that would never tan in the future. My hands moved as fast as possible and so did my mouth as I talked and repeated the motions over and over again. This job was better and I was making new friends. Thankfully I only needed one job to pay the bills, and that was my main concern.

Nela Park, the big lighting plant in Cleveland, had shut down lamp production. In order to keep their jobs, many of the workers transferred to Ravenna from the Cleveland area. I especially liked two ladies, Mary and Ivana, who came from Nela Park Lighting and were both originally from Slovenia. I loved hearing their foreign accents as they talked. They both had a unique sense of humor and baked the best strudel and baklava ever. It was a delight when they brought in these traditional Slovenian treats to share with us.

One Saturday afternoon Mary and I sat in the back room working overtime assembling the arc tube mounts. We had volunteered to work on a Saturday and nobody else wanted to work that day. It was just us and we had run out of small talk. I liked Mary with her red hair, freckles and fun personality. To help pass the time, I decided to try one of Bott's ideas, a throwback from my Western Reserve days, and casually asked, "Mary, what was the worst thing that ever happened to you?"

She knit her brows together in concentration and then started telling me an amazing story of how she came to America from Slovenia. She was very thoughtful as she recounted how sad she was to leave Slovenia. She didn't want to leave her family, but because her parents knew people in America they thought it would be a good opportunity for her to go. Reluctantly, she boarded the ship with hardly any money and set sail for America, scared to death. Her story was fascinating and I wish that I could remember more details. What I can't forget was hearing the emotion in her voice as she told about traveling alone, leaving her family and her homeland of Slovenia to arrive in a strange place where she hardly knew anyone and didn't understand the language. Everything was so strange, she remembered, and she even thought "hot dogs" were real dogs. Her story had a happy ending, since she married a fellow Slovenian and they now had a lovely daughter. Mary's home was in America, but it was clear that she never stopped missing her life with her family in Slovenia.

The worst thing that happened to her was leaving her family and coming to America. That surprised me because I thought that everyone wanted to live here. We were the best country, right? I never really thought about how terrible it would be to leave your family behind until Mary told me her story. It opened my eyes to a new way to thinking, and after that afternoon conversation, Mary and I became close friends.

∞∞∞∞∞∞∞∞∞∞

Our plum job of spot welding mount frames together came to an abrupt end when General Electric decided to ship the arc tubes to Mexico for the hand assembly. Our supervisor Charlotte was sent to Mexico to train the Mexican workers. When she came back, she told us that GE paid the Mexican workers in cash each week, and if I remember right, they earned about a dollar an hour. At that time, in the '80s, it cost less to ship the work to Mexico and back rather than pay workers the higher wage in the U.S. Gasoline was cheap. We had no choice but to accept the fact that the hand mounting jobs were being farmed out from under us.

Unfortunately, not long after that, I was laid off. I had only worked at GE for a year. Of course I applied for unemployment, but that was hardly enough to maintain my bills. It looked like I needed to seek different employment yet again and I didn't really want to return to the racetrack.

Although I would miss my paycheck from GE, in another way I was glad to be laid off. Working second shift at GE meant that I left my youngest son Adam home alone each evening. When I worked second shift, to ease my conscience about Adam staying alone, I got up early each morning and made him breakfast. This was the only time I'd see him for the rest of the day. Then I'd call him from work on my first break and at lunch.

My oldest son Earl still lived at home, but was usually not at home. He didn't like school and ended up quitting as soon as he was eighteen. He spent much of his time out in Freedom Township with his friends. Earl liked the country and usually worked for farmers on their corn or dairy farms. Fortunately, Adam was a trustworthy kid and spent most of his time playing on the computer, watching TV or reading. Still, I missed spending time with my son, so the lay-off gave me the chance to be home in the evenings.

It wasn't long after my lay off before an opportunity for a new job appeared, but surprisingly not from Betty. This time the opportunity came from her husband who was a beer salesman. He knew of a bar owner in Kent who wanted to hire a part-time, day-time barmaid. This job would be just right to supplement my unemployment and I could then be home in the evenings with Adam. So the job train switched tracks and jumped to a new rail line. And that's how I happened to become a bartender or barmaid, whatever you want to call it, which became my next job.

G.H. Ashenfelter

Job 13 – Lindy's Bar

The room was dim and smoky, unfamiliar faces moved in a blur around me. It was my first Saturday afternoon as a bartender and the little corner tavern was packed. Rushing to keep up with the drink demands, I filled and refilled numerous mugs of draft beer and tipped each glass sideways to keep the foam down, a lesson newly learned. My mind whirled and my back ached as I reached into the sweaty depths of the coolers and grabbed hold of the long necks of beer bottles, popped the caps off and slammed them up on the wooden bar. I collected the money and moved on to the next customer. This was a shot and a beer bar and the pace was fast.

It was amazing how much beer could be consumed in one afternoon. The mingling voices and laughter of the local crowd created an off key accompaniment to the loud music from the jukebox, a totally different background noise than what I was used to hearing in the factory. This small bar in Kent was the last place I expected to be working after landing that great paying job at GE. But, as usual, circumstances changed and again I needed extra money to pay the bills - any job was better than nothing. I served up drinks as fast as I could move and told myself, I can do this, which had become my main mantra for many jobs.

A nice shy-looking younger man with sandy, red hair approached the crowded bar and I recognized him as Sam. I had recently taken his order and collected the money for his first draft beer. "I'll have a Pabst Blue Ribbon draft," he requested quietly with a smile. I had just waited on him, so I smiled back and replied, "Another one already?" As soon as the words left my mouth, the place exploded with laughter. I looked around to see what caused the outburst and realized everyone was looking straight at me. They saw the confusion in my expression because another customer yelled out, "You never even got him the first beer, but you collected the money anyway." I then realized that Sam was probably too shy to tell me this himself. I tried to stutter an apology, but the place was in an uproar about the naïve and funny new barmaid. They were having a fun time at my expense and loving it. I knew they meant no harm, but my face burned bright red from embarrassment. In a neighborhood bar the regulars knew each other well. I was the newcomer and they were having a good laugh on me.

I worked days at the bar, which were not too busy and that suited me perfectly. I could be home evenings. It was a nice break from working second shift at GE. A typical day at the bar would start at

9:00 a.m., not that early. I would arrive, unlock the door, take my last breath of fresh air and enter. The stench of stale beer and cigarette smoke would hit me as I walked into the dimly lit room. Why don't bars have more windows, I wondered? The wooden chairs were piled upside down on the tables and their legs waved a tired good morning to me. I greeted them with a sigh as I flipped on the lights, filled the heavy mop bucket with hot sudsy water and started in on the floors. I liked to mop the floors. I'd drop some coins in the jukebox and punch the numbers to play Led Zeppelin's "Rock and Roll." The jukebox blared to life as the drums started the beat. I danced around the tables with the mop and sang along at the top of my lungs, "It's been a long time since I rock and rolled." This became a ritual at the beginning of each day - dancing with the mop to rock and roll.

Then chairs were lifted down in place and I moved on to clean the bathrooms, men's and women's. I was not thrilled with those duties, especially cleaning the men's room. I had to hold my breath so I didn't gag at the nasty urinal. I had never been in a men's bathroom before and the urinal was an unpleasant surprise. Gross and nauseating! But, I completed the chore. That unpleasant part out of the way, the bar officially opened at 10:00 for early drinkers and lunch.

The day manager at the bar, Mattie, arrived shortly after 10:00, drank her morning coffee and then went to work preparing the small kitchen to serve lunch. She did most of the cooking and always kept an upbeat attitude. We became friends right away. Mattie was maybe in her forties, nice looking, with high cheek bones, dark hair and a smile for everyone. She pretty much knew everyone in the neighborhood bar, and because of her, working as a barmaid turned out to be better than I expected. The work was fast paced, like GE, but never boring

Later in the afternoon the regulars, workers from Davey Tree, stopped in and tried to drink their weight in beer. One of the younger men from Davey Tree, Joe, had a crush on Mattie. They dated and as it turned out later, they ended up getting married. It was a real May/December romance and as far as I know, they are still together.

When I got to know the Davey guys better, I worried about them and their drinking habits. Often, when they stayed at the bar late, their wives would start calling for them to come home. They knew exactly where their husbands were. When the phone rang, the guys put their fingers to their lips and shook their heads no to urge me to say they were not there. Of course, the barmaid was expected to cover for the regulars, so I did, but I felt guilty about lying.

I wrote a country song for them called "One More," because that is what they would always say before they "finally" decided it was time to go home . . . "One more, one last one. He can't leave now cause he's havin' such fun. But she sits at home and waits by the phone, while he says I'll have just one more." My sad country ballad had no influence on getting them to go home to their wives any earlier.

G.H. Ashenfelter

The bar owner, Robert, a tall, handsome Irish man in his forties was an ex-boxer with full sandy-colored hair and dimples - a real ladies-man, according to his reputation. My daughters warned me never to go out with him and I had no intention of doing anything of the sort. He was my new boss and I didn't want to mess up that relationship. It was funny, in spite of this playboy reputation, he never made any unwanted advances toward me and I felt comfortable around him, no bad vibes. When I learned that Robert's apartment was right above the bar, I realized that he was upstairs sleeping in the mornings when I mopped. Oh, my, I'd better ask him if it was okay to play the jukebox full blast so early. When I mentioned this, he laughed heartily and told me to go right ahead and play the jukebox, he didn't even hear it. He must have been a sound sleeper.

My hours at the bar were 9:00 to 5:00, but the few times when I had to work nights, I felt better knowing that Robert was right up the stairs in case there was any trouble. From past experiences, I knew that alcohol, especially Jack Daniels, could cause people to turn mean and want to fight, but everyone respected Robert and knew he would not tolerate fighting. I often wondered if his boxing past deterred them.

One night when I had to work and knew he was not going to be upstairs, I expressed my fears about working alone that night. He told me if anyone caused any trouble to call him up and he would yell at them. Then he gave me that silly Irish grin, so what could I say to that?

Luckily, I never had to deal with any fights, only sad love spats. Robert worked hard at his business and he expected us to work hard - and I did. He used to say that nobody would need to diet if they just did real work. And it was true for me. All the time I worked there, I never had to diet - and I never went out with Robert.

Working at a bar offered other unique experiences like throwing darts and making up drink concoctions. The bar held dart tournaments and I soon got the knack of how to keep score along with keeping glasses full. By and by, I learned how to throw darts and bought my own set of sharp steel-tipped darts to join some of the tournaments. It was serious fun and games at the bar. I could easily get used to this life style.

On Saturday mornings, another delightful diversion was flirting with Ed, an owner of a bar down the street. Early Saturday mornings, he would come in to the bar and we would make up new drinks and try out different flavors of schnapps in milkshakes. They were tasty. In my opinion, Ed was handsome enough to play a lead part in a movie, and looked like a young James Garner. I had a small crush on him. We would laugh and joke, but he never asked me out. That's okay though, I would have said no because at that time I was seeing someone else. Yes, I had been divorced long enough to begin dating. Unfortunately, I did not pick out the most "eligible" men to date when I worked at the bar. They were too young or too married or drank too much. You name it.

One day a customer at the bar was reading palms and I asked him to read my palm. He said I could ask him one question. I thought about it for a moment and then asked, "Would I ever get married again?"

He held my hand and studied my palm careful. Finally he looked up and said, "No, you will not get married again, but you won't really mind." I pulled back my hand with a jolt - his answer stung me like a wasp. I was only in my forties, and thought for sure that I would marry again someday. But it wasn't in the cards or the palm for me to remarry. Was it my destiny? Well, call it what you will, but the prediction remained true.

Time passed by in a smoky haze as I continued to work as a barmaid at the little bar in Kent. The regulars stopped playing jokes on me now that I was wise to their humor. They couldn't get me with the old telephone joke. Larry would go into the phone booth and call the bar phone. When I answered, he asked me if Mike Hunt was there. Did you ever try yelling out "is Mike Hunt here" in a crowded bar? Don't do it! It's very embarrassing! Of course the whole bar would erupt with uncontrolled laughter. I yelled at Larry, yet I couldn't help but grin at their childish fun, shake my head and pour another beer.

It was easy to fall into the lifestyle of drinking, laughing at jokes and playing darts to pass the time. Bar life became comfortable, but I didn't want to remain a barmaid forever. Instinctively I knew that tending bar could not be a long term position for me and I had to find another way to make a living. But what could that be?

A year was up and I had just about given up hope of going back to GE. My unemployment was about to run out. I started searching for a more permanent type of job and spotted an ad in the local paper for a police dispatcher at the Streetsboro Police Department. Aha! This might be a good fit for a barmaid, I thought ironically, and decided to try for it.

There were umpteen hoops to jump through to apply for a police dispatcher position. They included numerous interviews, a typing test, a Civil Service Test, and even a lie detector test. I bought a book and studied for the Civil Service Test. Then I practiced my typing and got up to 35 words per minute. Somehow, I made it through the numerous interviews, but the lie detector test was unnerving. Hooked up to that machine, even when I told the truth, I felt like it was a lie.

When the results of my Civil Service Test came back, I was excited to find out that I had scored high on the test. As it turned out, I was one of two applicants who were eligible for the position. I must have aced that lie detector test. So now they just had to pick one of us.

G.H. Ashenfelter

Before I knew the final decision, fate barged in and I was called back to good old Generous Electric. I wavered, but only for a second. No doubt, for security and peace of mind, I had to return to my high paying factory job with benefits, and so I did. Thus began the second part of my life at GE.

To My So-called Old Loves

You really knew the worst of me,
The ugly side so rough.
The side that was so
Bold and bad and acted
Oh, so tough

You never knew the real of me
That slid down out of sight.
You only knew the other side
That came out
Late at night.

The insecure and not real pure,
That primal side revealed.
The other side that could
Be harmed was
Stealthily concealed.

You had the measure and the part
Of me that didn't have a heart.
That acted like it was alive,
But really,
I slept deep inside.

G.H. Ashenfelter

Job 12 – General Electric Continued – Part 2

Leaving my bar life behind with its fun-loving people and constant social activity was difficult at first. I missed it on many levels, but knew it was the right thing to move on. Back on the factory line again, my hands did the repetitive motions and the bulbs went round and round for eight long hours. This had to be my life now and I accepted it.

GE workers were required to learn all the jobs on the lines so that we could rotate positions, an idea developed to help prevent repetitive motion injuries. Many of the women who worked at GE showed me the scars on their wrists from the carpal tunnel surgeries. My head would shake back and forth in sympathy, but in my mind I was hoping that wouldn't happen to my hands.

One position on the line that I detested was running the basing wheel, the last machine at the end where the metal bases were screwed on to finish up the bulbs. It was difficult for me to twist the metal bases on straight and keep up with the machine. Men seemed to be more proficient on the basing wheel, so maybe it was a hand and arm strength issue. I only know my wrists and arms ached after that job. I preferred the tipping position on the exhaust machine using the little torch to seal the air inside the lamps. Ultimately my main goal was to get off the big line as soon as possible.

I was waiting for an open position to become available on the Line Two Mount Machine so I could work with my friend Connie again. The mount machine was a new, automated machine that automatically, robotically, welded together the arc tube mounts, the same ones we used to assemble and weld by hand when I first started at GE - the hand assembly job that went south to Mexico.

Even though workers had to move their hands fast to load parts on the mount machine, it was a smaller range of motion and far easier than working on the big line, plus workers could talk to each other. Time sped up in direct proportion to how much we could talk. Finally, the much desired position on the mount machine came up for bid and I had enough seniority to get that position.

GE was very progressive. They allowed workers to bid on new jobs and the person with the highest seniority should win the bid. To be fair, every worker's seniority date and pay amount was posted right on the bulletin board. When the position came open for the line two mount machine, I bid on it immediately and hoped for the best.

What happened then both surprised me, and made me angry. A new girl was hired and assigned to the mount machine, the very job I had bid on. When I found out she was the foreman's daughter I had steam coming out of my ears like a character in an old cartoon. Confrontation frightened me, but fair was fair at GE. Every worker knew that!

With indignant righteousness, I marched up to the main office and complained, I mean stated my case. I had placed a bid on the mount machine job and someone with less, even no seniority was working there. To my satisfaction, they agreed it was wrong. But before I could move to the mount machine, I had to train the new girl, the foreman's daughter, on the big line. Needless to say, I was not thrilled about that. Since her dad was a foreman, I was sure she knew I was the one who got her kicked off the cushy mount machine job.

Nevertheless, I was proud since this was the first time that I actively stuck up for myself on a job. That was what workers did at GE. This was not Western Reserve Electronics where I just did what I was told to do, no questions or complaints. Maybe being a line leader or barmaid had changed me in some positive ways.

The foreman's daughter, Carol, showed up on the big line for training the next afternoon. She was younger than me, probably about the age of my daughters, and was friendly, but I was a bit leery. It didn't take long for me to realize that Carol was a nice person and not one bit upset about losing the mount machine position. I was relieved about that and started to relax. As we moved the huge light bulbs from basket to machine and back into baskets, I found out that we had some things in common. We both liked reading, we both played the piano and we both liked learning. She explained that she wanted to go to college, and then I confided that so did I, some day. Where did that come from? Did I really want to go to college? As the shift progressed, I decided to be honest and told Carol how I was responsible for her ending up on the big line. She just laughed and said that it was only fair.

Suddenly the work was lighter. After two weeks of training together, we became fast friends. When the training ended, I was sorry about leaving the big line because I would miss Carol's company. Still, off I went to the mount machine position that I had fought so hard to win. Being able to move to different jobs and earn the same money as your peers, whether you were a woman or a man, gave me a positive feeling. I liked being an employee at this big corporation and even though we had no union, we followed union rules.

GE was a great place to earn a living even if the repetitive motions often dulled your senses or injured your wrists. There was a rhythm to this job - the bell rang, we started work, the bell rang, we had a coffee break, the bell rang, we had lunch and finally the bell rang to end our day. If there was nobody to talk to, I memorized song lyrics and sang them over and over; it was better than thinking about my past mistakes in life that couldn't be fixed. Sometimes, even singing didn't help speed up my shift. One night I watched the clock on the far wall, anxious for my break. The stubborn hands would not move, in fact, they sometimes waved at me in a mocking gesture. In retaliation, I would make a face and stick my tongue out at the fixed hands, and believe it or not, the hands would jump backwards. I guess that time is relevant, Mr. Einstein.

Fortunately, an opportunity came up that helped keep my mind from slipping a cog. I teamed up with Carol and we joined the newly formed Communication Council at GE. This council helped plan and write a small monthly newsletter about the lamp plant and its employees. Another friend from the line, Dana, a highly motivated young lady, was the appointed secretary and editor. Carol and I were the roving reporters. We worked well together and the planning meetings were a "highlight" for me. The *Ravenna Lamp Highlights – Dedicated to Lighting the World* included informative articles about changes in the lighting industry, employee pictures, and recent news about the employees and their families. Each June, we honored high school or college graduates, sons and daughters of our employees. In addition, we interviewed and wrote articles about newly hired workers. Each Christmas we compiled recipes submitted by workers into a little recipe booklet.

The newsletter was a big hit at the plant. We were allowed some time away from our jobs one day a week to brainstorm ideas. This newsletter was my first real attempt at writing for a specific audience, namely our fellow lamp plant workers. Being on the Communication Council gave me added confidence and eventually helped lead to my decision to begin taking classes at Kent State University using the Individual Development Program, a benefit that was offered by our company

Even though I'm not writing about my personal life, I will say that I was stumbling along with different boyfriends. Up to this time, I thought that maybe I would find someone, in spite of the palm reader's prediction. Friends said I was too independent or too picky. I wasn't too picky - I just picked the most unsuitable men, or maybe they picked me. Perhaps it was a blessing in disguise when I broke up with my last "real" boyfriend. Or should I say that he broke up with me. Nevertheless, I had vowed that I was never going to cry over men again, but I did cry for three days. Then I picked myself up, brushed myself off and enrolled in college. That breakup and my work on the Communication Council was my catalyst to begin taking classes.

Since my divorce, I consoled and healed myself with self-help books and quotes. These books were my counselors. One quote by T.H. White from *The Once and future King* made a huge impact on me about education.

> *"The best thing for being sad," replied Merlin, beginning to puff and blow, "is to learn something. That's the only thing that never fails."*

That quote settled it. I would listen to Merlin and learn "why the world wags and what wags it." However, I was not sure of my ability to handle college courses and the academic life. I did not feel especially bright after making light bulbs the live long day, but still hoped that my brain was not totally dim.

I took advantage of the "Individual Development Program" offered by my company - good old Generous Electric. I paid for my first class. The program would reimburse the tuition when, or if, the employee passed the class with a C or better. I could do this, I thought, and so began an academic journey that lasted nine years. From 1990 to 1998, I went to college part time and worked full time making light bulbs.

I started out with one class, Sociology 101, and discovered that I had a passion for the campus atmosphere, meeting other students and reading - studying and reading was my new vocation. I embraced it. Reading books had always been major part of my life, so I loved the fact that going to college required me to read even more books. Each class was new and different and it gave me something to think about as I assembled, packed or inspected the GE lamps. I was excited about college, even though some of my co-workers and family members thought I was wasting my time getting an education since I already had a secure job. But I kept going.

∞∞∞∞∞∞∞∞∞∞

20 Jobs: A Memoir

As a kid, I was often draped over a chair in our living room with a comic book or paperback book balanced on my knees. The overstuffed chair was blue and scratchy, but this did not distract me from the written words on the page. I was off in another world, my own world in my own mind. No other family member in my household read books. My dad read the newspaper every night, but I never saw my mom read anything except recipes. My two sisters and brother never caught the reading bug either. I don't know where I got this love of reading.

My older sister Betty, who bragged that she never read a book, would walk by the chair, smack my leg and yell at me to get off my lazy butt. "Do something," she yelled, "clean up this messy house." I looked up from my book and gave her a dirty look. I wasn't about to stop reading no matter how lazy she thought I was.

∞∞∞∞∞∞∞∞∞∞

But look at me now, in college, where reading and studying was required. My backpack full of books never left my side and at work I read on breaks and during lunch - so proud to be a student. My dark blue Kent State backpack was a symbol of my ongoing education. They could not call me lazy for reading now.

An added bonus of attending Kent State was that my son, Adam, was also in college during this same time period and drove bus for Campus Bus Service. Since I worked second shift, I took classes during the day and often rode Adam's bus to campus. How fun it was to watch him wield that large bus around the corners with skill and ease. Mom and son going to college at the same time and he was doing the driving. We often met at the Student Center for lunch and my nine years studying at Kent State were some of my happiest, and busiest, years.

I started out as an English major and eventually added Secondary Education to my courses. In the year 1998, I graduated from Kent State University Magna Cum Laude with my degree in English and Secondary Education. I have to admit that I didn't start out trying to graduate with honors, but once I began earning A's and B's, I worked hard to keep the momentum. My son Adam graduated one year before me with his degree in computer programming and he played a big part in my decision to leave the factory.

At General Electric, the glass bulbs rolled down the lines for 13 years as I rotated through at least 20 different jobs inside the factory. I worked on four lines, on the mount machine and basing wheel, in the environmental room making arc tubes, in central pack, in the stem machine department and in Hal-I-R as an inspector of halogen lights. I saw robotics enter our workplace and replace workers one by one. I saw some catastrophes.

The Environmental room where the arc tubes were made was separated from the rest of the plant. It was the only room with air conditioning and a coveted job. We walked by the glassed in room and peered through the windows to see the workers sitting in cool comfort. Some even wore sweaters. A hand-made sign on the window would read: "Inside 72 degrees – outside 98 degrees" We were all envious until the day the ceiling fans malfunctioned and the room was shut down. Thorium, which I knew nothing about at the time, had backed up into the room and polluted the environment inside. I later learned that thorium is a naturally-occurring, slightly radioactive metal discovered in 1828 by the Swedish chemist Jons Jakob Berzelius, who named it after Thor, the Norse god of thunder. Thorium is found in small amounts in most rocks and soils, and I guess it was found in our environmental room too.

Workers stared as men in sealed white suits complete with head gear walked through our plant and into the polluted room to clean up the thorium. Soon after that, all the workers had to be tested for exposure. Now the environmental room did not seem to be such a desirable job. Next the company tested us for mercury poisoning. Many of the arc tubes contained mercury and often broke spilling out the silver substance. Now I was beginning to wonder exactly what we were exposed to at GE.

I worked second shift, first shift and even night shift to pick up some required classes. Night shift was the worst! I can remember falling asleep standing up on the job. I only realized that I was asleep because suddenly it was quiet - the noise in the shop had faded away. It scared me as I jerked myself awake and immediately left the floor, break or no break, to get a cup of coffee. I wanted to get off that shift as soon as possible.

During those years at GE, I grew in many ways. I built my credit back up and bought a little house on the west side of Kent, close to the bus line for Adam. I started to believe in myself more. Perhaps this self assurance came from attending college and from working with a wide variety of people in so many different job situations. I found that I could still learn new things at my ripe old age. But now I was faced with some big questions: Was I ready to move forward into a new profession? Could I become a teacher? Would I have the guts to quit my secure job?

Before I could finish my Secondary Education Degree, I was required to do student teaching. My education degree was for grades 7 through 12, and it worried me constantly about whether I could get a position teaching at a middle school or high school when I was already 55 years old. Only one way to find out! In the spring of my graduation year, I quit my good paying job at GE to student teach at Mantua Middle School and get my teaching certificate.

It was a bold and scary move and pretty much unheard of for anyone to quit GE, one of the most coveted jobs for pay and benefits in our area. It was just not done. There were only two people that I knew of who quit our plant. One was Dana, my young co-worker from the communication council.

She left and found an office position at our local hospital. Another woman, Cindy, studied for a real estate license and then left to sell homes. To my knowledge, they were the only two workers who made this giant leap of faith and quit Generous Electric. Now I was the third.

This decision to quit was painfully difficult, but I was at a crossroad in my life. Either I stayed in the factory and made light bulbs till I retired, or moved on to a new challenge. I chose to move on even though I wondered if I was a fool for making that choice. It was an internal struggle, but what is that old saying? No pain, no gain? Or is it no job, no pay? Whatever the consequences, I had to try.

Fortunately, my son Adam believed in me. He had graduated in 1997 and was currently working at the Cleveland Plain Dealer in Cleveland. When I asked for his help, he didn't hesitate as he stepped up to take over the house payment and utility bills until I could "hopefully" find employment at a school in the fall. I'm not sure I would have quit GE without his support.

Retirees from General Electric received a huge multi-vapor lamp mounted on a base and stuffed with money. I wasn't retiring, but my co-workers lovingly made me a multi-vapor lamp and stuffed it with flowers. The base contained a little gold plaque engraved with my name, the date I started at GE and the date I quit.

G.H. Ashenfelter

Gladys Ashenfelter
7/12/1984 – 2/27/1998

I worked at General Electric for thirteen and half years. This was the longest that I ever stayed at one job and it was difficult to say goodbye to my co-workers. I was overwhelmed and touched by their kindness. My department threw me a little farewell party and a co-worker, Peggy, made me a funny photo album as a keepsake. Ivana was there and I'm sure she brought strudel, but sadly, my friend Mary who told me her story about her trip to America from Slovenia was not there to see me off to a new life apart from GE.

Before I graduated, Mary got the dreaded cancer and passed away. I was devastated to lose her. She had always encouraged me to pursue my education and was proud of me for going to school. I wished that she could have been there. Goodbyes to dear friends are the worst part of moving on.

∞∞∞∞∞∞∞∞∞∞∞∞

After my student teaching was completed, I psyched-up to find a position as a teacher. To beef up my résumé, I volunteered as a tour guide at Stan Hywet Hall and Gardens and guided groups through the Seiberling mansion in Akron. Also I joined a bell choir and a singing choir at a local church in Cuyahoga Falls. If I was going to become a teacher, I wanted to get more involved in the community, especially since I would no longer be working a second shift job and would have evenings free.

My family was expanding and along with my two granddaughters, April and Melissa, I had a new grandson. My daughter Earlene had her first son, Michael. I looked forward to spending some summer time days with my grandchildren. I also looked forward to a summer free from sweaty afternoon shifts at GE.

On the downside, summer was looking bleak with no extra money coming in, but just in time an opportunity for a summer job as a secretary in a mobile home park appeared. My sister was responsible for this job opportunity, but not Betty. This time it was my younger sister Jane. She and her husband Ray managed and owned mobile home parks out in Beloit. Jane hired me as a summer office assistant. Looking back, I'm positive that this was more to help me than it was to help her.

Job 14 – Trailer Park office Assistant

Oh, the joy of summertime freedom; something I had not experienced in a long, long time. For the past 12 years I worked full time at GE and for the last nine of those years I went to college to earn my Bachelor's Degree in English and Secondary Education. Not much spare time on that schedule. I felt like a kid on the first day of summer vacation as I drove east on Route 14 past the local fruit stand and green open fields. It was a balmy June day and the breeze blew through my hair as the oldies blasted on the radio. It's summer time and the livin' is easy, I sang with glee - no more sweating it out on the GE Multi-Vapor line. I was on my way for the first day of work for my sister Jane at the trailer park she managed in Beloit.

I would not miss summers at GE. Working 2nd shift on long summer evenings, I saw only machines, glass bulbs and walls. There were no windows in our plant and I longed to be home and sit outside to watch the afternoon light fade slowly into evening blues and pinks. But instead, I was stuck on the hot line. Sometimes at work I ate supper outside on the picnic table, or stepped out for a quick five minutes of fresh air, but there was no time to waste in a 24 minute lunch break.

Back inside on the factory floor, temperatures often reached 90 to a 100 degrees, and sometimes hotter. Because of the intense heat, I guzzled Gatorade, ate popsicles and placed wet towels around my neck. Hot air piped in from outside blew directly on my face and dried the sweat on my clothes, no air conditioning. Summer livin' was not easy at GE.

But I missed the people I worked with, especially Mary, who lost her battle with cancer. I thought about her often. I knew she would be proud of me if she knew that I had graduated from college and was about to begin a new future, even if facing that future was like stepping out on thin ice - not sure if it would hold me or not. The factory floor was behind me along with the stable paycheck and benefits! The part time job as my sister Jane's office assistant would have to see me through till I found a position in teaching.

As I pulled up and parked by Jane's double wide trailer, I was a little apprehensive as to what she would want me to do. She came out and greeted me with a business like friendliness and offered me a cup of coffee. She always had the coffee pot on. She and her husband Ray had as many as four parks to maintain and manage. In addition, Jane sold mobile homes on the side.

G.H. Ashenfelter

We sipped our coffee and Jane spent about an hour explaining more about her businesses and her routine. I was confused about the exact nature of my new work, but being the older sister by 11 years, I was not going to act confused. There was, after all, family dynamics to consider. I was supposed to be top dog in the sister department, but my little sister was now my boss. Step lightly, I told myself.

Until my brother Joe was born when I was nine years old, I had been the baby of the family. Jane came along two years later when I was eleven years old. When Joe and Jane were growing up, Dad and Mom went through a divorce. Dad remarried, so Joe and Jane had a step-mother and two step-brothers. It was difficult to blend the families. By the time Joe and Jane were teens, I was married and living in my own home with kids. They came out to stay with us during the summers and on many weekends. I especially liked having my little sister stay with me because it felt like she was one of my kids. I sewed Barbie doll clothes for her and we made lots of cookies together. I was the mother figure and boss to my little sister Jane, but now the tables were turned and I was going to work for her.

Jane had a set system of how she did everything. It was soon apparent that her way was the right way and basically the only way. I respected that, adjusted to her routine and did the job exactly as she asked me to. Some of my duties were writing letters to collect rents, writing checks, filing and mailing bills. Jane did learn some computer skills from me when I taught her how to save business letters. It saved some time. Looking back, I cannot remember exactly what else I did as my sister's office assistant.

We visited over coffee often and Jane probably could have done my duties in half the time it took me to complete them. Still, when she was busy, I was there to answer the phone and do some typing. I hope that helped her out. In my heart, I knew she was doing me a favor by hiring me as her assistant. The extra pay enabled me to make it financially through the summer and I appreciated that. But I'm not sure I really assisted her that much with her office work.

My other main task that summer was applying for positions at schools within a thirty mile radius. A teaching position would not come looking for me. I had to go in hot pursuit. When I wasn't working for Jane, I sat and worked on my computer in the basement. I thought it would be a breeze to complete school applications, but after awhile I wondered who wrote them. Were they designed by bureaucratic, sadistic, test writers? Some applications took me hours to complete. Along with the contact information that applications demanded, they asked applicants to answer three or four short essay questions. But, the answers were never short. For instance, "Give three reasons that you want to become a teacher," or "What are your five strengths and weaknesses? (You may use the back of the paper if you run out of room)."

In the late '90s, most applications had to be hand written and then mailed to the schools. It was tiresome. I began keeping copies of the applications and using the same answers, or variations of the answers, to fit different questions. After awhile, on paper, I sounded pretty terrific, even to myself. I was dependable, smart, talented, and creative along with any other adjectives that extolled my virtues. I filled the empty spaces with verbiage dedicated to me. After all this, I reasoned, some school district will have to hire me.

My summer of freedom was almost over. In August I had a couple of interviews, even one at Akron City Schools, but no direct promise of a teaching position. My résumé and grades looked impressive, and I hid my age on applications, 55. But in a face to face interview my age was difficult to hide. I know many principals were shocked to see an older, recent college graduate in low pump heels and a boxy, unfashionable suit walk into their office. I could see it on their faces even as they tried to hide their surprise. But I was not going to be discouraged. I had come too far to go back.

A breakthrough came when I attended a job fair at Cuyahoga Falls and interviewed with a variety of school principals and superintendents. A principal from Cuyahoga Falls High School, Ed Holland, was very interested in the fact that I was up to date about computer programs like Word and Excel - thank you, Adam, for loving computers and for making me use them.

My job future was looking more promising when they called me to come for an interview at Cuyahoga Falls. Arriving at the school, I interviewed with Mr. Holland again. He explained that they were looking for a teacher to work in their new computer writing center. Because of my English degree and recent experience with computer programs, I qualified for this new opening. My second interview went well, and I was hired in spite of my age. I was super excited about working at a high school and anxious to begin a new career and a new chapter in my life story.

G.H. Ashenfelter

Job 15 - Cuyahoga Falls High School

When my job fair interview landed me the teaching position at Cuyahoga Falls High School, I was sleepless with visions of classrooms dancing in my head. Was it possible that this year, the fall of 1998, would be the best year of my life? I was sure it would. My new classroom would be academic but welcoming, the walls lined with artful and stimulating posters. My windows would look out over great rolling, dew covered lawns complete with blossoming trees to inspire the students. Lessons would be fun and stimulating, and of course, I would be in control of unruly students at all times. Many of my classes in college were aimed at class management and focused on how to keep students engaged throughout the day.

I had put those ideas into practice during my student teaching at Crestwood Middle School. Of course the experienced classroom teacher, Mrs. Paul was always close by, so that probably deterred any bad behavior. But I had learned so much from preparing lessons and managing a classroom. I felt ready to guide students to inspirational, educational heights. Otherwise, I was full of myself.

In 1998, Cuyahoga Falls High School was a city school with around 2,500 students. The building had two main parts, the three-story tall original brick building in the back and the new addition built in the front that included offices for the principals and guidance department, the grand auditorium, spacious cafeteria/gym, and the vocational wing for business, automotive and beautician classes.

This sprawling school building loomed in front of me as I walked up to the main entrance a week before the first day of classes to find and prepare my classroom. I entered through the front door of the new building and found the main office down the hall to the left. Feeling nervous, I stood by the tall counter where a secretary was seated at her desk. I cleared my throat to catch her attention. I glanced to the left where cubby-hole teacher mailboxes lined the wall. I peered over. Was my name on there yet? The secretary who had "Jane" written on her name tag looked up expectantly at me.

"Hi," I said, "I'm Gladys Ashenfelter the new writing center teacher. I'm here to prepare my classroom."

Jane fit the part of school secretary with her stylish glasses and neatly bobbed short blond hair. She smiled, "Nice to meet you, Gladys. Give me a minute and I'll walk you up to your room."

"Thanks," I replied, as I flashed back my new winning, professional smile. Even I knew it was important to be in good graces with the principal's secretary and was eager to make a strong first impression. I wanted Jane to like me. I found out later that I could have relaxed, because Jane liked everyone. She was the perfect representative for our high school office, a very caring individual who was respectful to adults and students alike.

I followed Jane as she walked briskly up the broad main hallway and past the library. Our footsteps echoed in the empty halls and I wondered why I couldn't just find my room by myself. As we continued up several flights of stairs and around a maze of corners, I soon knew why. I was completely lost. Finally, we came to my room that was at the far end hallway on the third floor. I found out later we were in the old building. It was as far from the main office as you could get.

When Jane opened the door to room 326, my eyes widened in surprise. Inside was a little narrow space that was more like a large hallway. There was a door at each end of the room, and to my dismay, no windows. Three round tables filled the middle of the room and looked like they could each accommodate five or six students. Along the walls, large desk-top computers sprouting assorted cords sat on top of ugly brown metal desks. They were in sad disarray looking like they had lost their connections to their last homes. The room had a bookcase with four shelves, but no teacher desk in sight. Trying to hide my disappointment, I smiled and muttered a quick "Thanks" to Jane. Suddenly she was in a hurry as she turned abruptly and left me alone with the tangled mess of cords and dejected computers. I didn't know where to begin and was disappointed to find out that the room didn't have windows or a teacher's desk. Where would a desk fit in that little room even if I found one?

The hallways were quiet. Warily, I walked across my new room and through the far door only to discover that my room was connected to what must be the teachers' lounge with two large rectangular tables, long counters, spacious cupboards, a microwave, and a refrigerator. Attached to the lounge were some side rooms for storage and a room with a copy machine. In truth, the lounge was bigger and nicer than my room. Having the teachers' lounge next to my room would be handy to access the copy machine and to eat lunch, I thought, which is exactly what every teacher thought. Out of habit, teachers and aides had used my once empty room as a short cut through to the teachers' lounge and copier. A habit that was hard to break, I soon discovered.

I went out through the far door and into the hall. As I walked around the hallway, I discovered that it formed a square and I found myself right back by my door on the other side. The halls were quiet and deserted. What I didn't realize was that veteran teachers don't show up at school until a couple of days before classes, not a week before like me. But by the looks of things it would take at least a week to get the writing center room whipped into shape.

G.H. Ashenfelter

I heard a shuffling sound down the hall, ah people, and followed the noise to find if there was someone around. My footsteps echoed on the polished stone floor as I peered into each room until I discovered a lovely lady with blonde hair pulled up in a pony tail sitting at a desk. I introduced myself and found out her name was Melanie and she was head of the Special Education Department. She barely looked up from her work, and her actions made it clear that she was busy. Much to her dismay, I didn't leave and persisted in asking questions about the school and about where I could find a desk.

Probably to get rid of me, she gave up on her work and helped me look in empty rooms until we found a desk that no one was using - a big heavy metal, brown monstrosity. And it was filthy! There were old cigarette butts squashed in the corners of the top desk drawer. Yuck! How long had this thing been out of use? No matter, I'll take it. It was my first real teacher desk. Melanie helped me push and maneuver the desk into the writing center. It barely fit into the far corner of the room, and fortunately did not block the entrance door to the teachers' lounge. I angled it out a little so I could squeeze in behind it and there was just enough room for a chair, but first I had to find one. Mission accomplished. Melanie disappeared even faster than Jane had. I figured this was enough progress for one day.

The next day, I returned and found a small parking lot at the back of the school that was closer to my room. I hiked up the three flights of stairs with my cleaning supplies and spent the second day scouring the computer desks, tables and my teacher's desk with heavy duty cleaners, Clorox wipes and paper towels. I wrestled the heavy old Macintosh computers and screens into place. From the looks of the tangled mess of cords, I knew there was only one solution. I would have to use my special secret weapon, Adam, my computer geek son, to bring these computers back to life. After the thorough cleaning, the room was taking on a new glow for me. I left and went shopping to buy posters for the walls. I would need a bunch since there were no windows.

I was certain that Adam would help me on his Saturday off from the Plain Dealer, and I was right. He was proud of me for getting a teaching position and happy for me to take over the bills again. Adam and I arrived at the high school, entered through the back door and trudged up the three flights of stairs up to my room.

I unlocked and opened the door. "Well, what do you think, Adam?" I asked hopefully.

"Nice room." He answered and I wondered if he was being sarcastic.

But he didn't even flinch when he saw the mess of cords and acted like he was impressed with my little domain, even though it was not much to look at. Then he went into his leave-me-alone, nerd working mode and wrought his magic. In a couple of hours, he had the computers plugged in and working. When he turned them on, the computers lit up and put on their smiley faces. It was a miracle when the screens glowed with neon blue life. My room was now ready, thanks to Adam, but I was not sure if I was ready for my duties as a writing center teacher.

The third floor in the old building was home for the English department and the Special Education Unit at Cuyahoga Falls High School. A couple of days before classes began, the English teachers showed up to prepare their rooms. They were friendly, but busy, like Melanie. It was pretty apparent that I didn't really fit into their academic world at this time. I had trained as a teacher, but was hired for the writing center as a tutor, with the hourly pay of a tutor, which was considerably less than a teacher's pay. Because of my status as an ISGI, Individual Small Group Instructor, at first the English teachers didn't seem to consider me an equal, or a real classroom teacher. It took some time for this attitude to change.

In 1998, computers were very slow compared to today's high-speed computers, but they were used primarily for writing and printing papers, not so much for searching the Internet like they are today. The writing center position was a new job created to bring the high school up to date with more computer labs. My writing center was an experiment.

Keeping a simple journal about my life, here is the journal entry exactly as I wrote it that day:
Journal Entry Sept. 1, 1998

My first day with students. I miss having a classroom like when I did student teaching; I walk by and see the classes and am sort of sad. No literature, kids & so on. My little room is a busy thoroughfare; everyone cuts through into the teacher's lounge. I had 3 students, two were lost. Justin Im?? I took Justin to see about his schedule & then I had a kid who was determined to rearrange all the computers & find games. I finally got him interested in making a sign for my door. Observations: No black teachers, 1 black student. This is really strange. I typed and made lists and talked to people cutting through my room on their way to the lounge.

The fledgling writing center was off to a slow start and sometimes days passed by with not one serious student coming by to use the computers, except for Justin who took a liking to me since I helped him on the first day. He was a brilliant kid in the special education program, probably high functioning autistic, and he loved computers. Justin gravitated towards my writing center and came in at random times. Sometimes in a matter of minutes, he used every computer and had them in error mode or shut down. Don't ask me what he did. I just know it took me hours to get it undone. Pretty soon, I started limiting him to one computer that he always said didn't work.

Justin created a host of computer problems. In spite of this, I still liked him. He was sweet natured and well meaning; plus, he was my first student. For my sanity, I started to insist he bring a note from his teacher to visit the writing center. I think they just misplaced him at times. Fortunately, as the school year progressed, I acquired more students and the writing center evolved and grew.

New rule: students must have a note from their teachers to use the writing center. They also had to sign in on a daily log placed inside my door to show where they were during each period of the day. At the end of the day this log was sent down to the attendance office. A number of students whom teachers had habitually sent to the library were now sent to my room. Usually they were the troublemakers who talked too much or couldn't sit still. When these kids found out about the writing center, they became my main group of students in addition to Justin. My largest group, usually boys, but some girls, arrived during 6th and 7th periods when many students were just tired of sitting in the classroom and ready to go home. There was Barry, Tom, Samantha, Jack, and so on - I quickly learned that it was best to keep these kids busy, so I acquired a book tree and started stocking it with young adult books that I had acquired from my college classes or bought at garage sales.

If students didn't bring any work, I gave them a book to read and lent the books out to any student who wanted to read them. To my dismay, I lost many of my best books to forgetful students until I started keeping track of who borrowed what book and that helped, but not completely.

Our high school had a great library in the school, but it was a mile hike downstairs, so many students chose to get books from the writing center. Besides that, students told me that they had been kicked out of the library, probably for not returning books. As the year went on, my writing center evolved into a reading center and sanctuary for these restless kids. Soon it would evolve even more.

One afternoon, our assistant principal, Mrs. Cook, made a special trek up to the far corner of the third floor to meet with me for the first time. We hardly ever saw a principal this far from the main office, so I was wondering why she was interested in visiting the lowly writing center coordinator. It seems that Mrs. Cook was on a mission. Using her formal principal speaking voice, she patiently explained to me why the 9th Grade Proficiency Tests were extremely important to our school. Due to the importance of these tests, she had an extra special assignment just for me.

A red flag warning sprung up in my head. In our education classes at Kent, we often discussed proficiency testing. In the collegiate world, testing was considered a necessary evil. Here in the high school world, it was a number one top priority.

According to Mrs. Cook, her mission was now my mission. We had to find out which students did not pass the reading and the writing on the 9th grade proficiencies and then schedule them to come for tutoring in the writing center during their study hall. It sounded easy enough, but turned out to be a logistics nightmare. First off, I had to request the results of the tests from guidance, which they did not like to share since they were the keepers of the tests and very possessive about this information. Finally, after repeated attempts on my part, they shared the test results. Then, I had to learn to decipher those crazy test charts. Since Cuyahoga Falls was a large school, there were hundreds of names to go through and analyze. It took some time.

After figuring out which students had failed the reading or writing parts of the test, I looked up each student's class schedule to see if they had a study hall. Next, I found each student in their study halls and scheduled them for tutoring. They were required to come to the writing center instead of going to the study halls. After this lengthy process, I found out that students did not want to give up their study halls to come up to the little, out of the way writing center for proficiency tutoring. They hated the idea of losing their free time, so they would often not show up. Then, I hunted them down again in their study halls and enforced the tutoring, orders from principal headquarters. I was not so popular at first.

I embraced my new duties as a tutor for reading and writing proficiencies with the passion of a first year teacher. When I finally coerced the students into coming up to the writing center, I enjoyed working with them one-on-one. With direct interaction, I had the chance to get to know students better than I could in a conventional classroom. Getting along well with people, young and old, was a skill I learned from working in so many different situations and from taking classes in education.

One lesson demonstrated in my education classes at Kent State had a huge impact on me. This particular education class was taught by a lovely, wise teacher named Leslie. She knew about teaching since she was an actual, experienced high school teacher at Kent City Schools. Leslie stressed that students might forget what they learn, but they would never forget how they were treated. The discipline and atmosphere in your classroom was directly connected to this premise.

She demonstrated this idea in our class one day by having us play a game of poker. Four students were picked to play in the game while the rest of the class observed. I was one of the students who played and was given a large number of chips to start. Another player had fewer chips and two players were given only one or two chips. As the cards were dealt and we played each hand, I placed lots of bets since I could afford to win or lose chips and have plenty of chips left over. The students who started with one or two chips were very careful and did not take chances in case they lost their few chips and were taken out of the game. I noticed that they physically covered the chips with their hands as if to keep them safe. They placed very few bets because they couldn't afford to lose.

G.H. Ashenfelter

Afterwards, our teacher Leslie explained that this poker game was an analogy for students in the classroom. The chips represented each student's self esteem or confidence. If a student had many chips, or lots of self esteem, they could afford to lose chips and it would hardly affect them. If a student had one or two chips, or low self esteem, they held on to their chips for dear life. If you tried to take away the chips, or self esteem, they were very likely to hold them closer or even fight for them.

I never forgot this poker game analogy. It served me well working with teens. Respect for all students became my first rule as I remembered not to take away their chips. The best part of teaching for me was working with students - a common refrain, but in my case, it really was true.

As the year progressed, I began to wonder. How do you teach and evaluate writing? Not the 5-paragraph format or grammar rules, this I already knew, but the art of writing and the motivation to write. As I thought more and more about this, I remembered that Kent State had a writing center which, sad to say, I never visited in my nine years of college. I decided that finally it was time for a visit.

Kent State's writing center was hidden in a back hallway of the English building, like my writing center, small and tucked away. The staff was friendly and helpful and took extra time to walk me through a typical writing session. They even gave me some books to use to help evaluate a student's writing. After reading them, I realized that I needed to be careful when grading writing and not stomp all over a student's paper. Writing is so personal. A student might pour their heart out in an essay only to see it bleed red ink from the teacher comments. No wonder so many students think they are poor writers and are reluctant to write.

I decided to try a new approach from the Kent State Writing Center to teach writing in my writing center. On Monday, I tried it out on Amy who was my first writing student of the morning. She was tall and willow thin with long, straight blonde hair. She loved dancing and was a ballerina, but this morning she was my guinea pig writing student. To begin, I had her to write a first draft essay using a sample prompt from the Proficiency Test. The essay prompt asked a student to, "Tell a story about a time you took a vacation with your family or friends. Be sure to organize your writing into paragraphs and add lots of description." We read the prompt together, decided it was a narrative prompt and Amy started writing.

About twenty minutes later, she stopped writing and looked at me. I edged out from behind my desk, sat down beside her at the round table and asked her to read her paper out loud. She did and then I said, "It sounds like you had a nice time on your vacation. I like the way you organized your writing into five paragraphs and you did tell a story. She visibly relaxed and smiled at my praise, but was surprised when I said, "What kind of grade would you give your essay"? She looked at me for help, but I remained neutral.

"Well," she hedged, "I guess a D or C." I nodded and said, "That seems fair. I would probably give it a C. But why would you give it that grade?"

"I'm not sure." She replied. "Maybe I didn't add enough details?" I smiled for encouragement and kept reminding myself that writing is personal - it's her story so let her continue. "Yes, I think you could add more details to your story. Do you remember how to do that?"

Again Amy took a moment before answering, "Yes, I do remember! You look at the five senses of taste, touch, smell, feel, and sight." She was smiling now. "That's right!" I said, "Okay, I have one more suggestion. Look at the last paragraph and see if you can wrap up your story a little better, it just kind of stops in mid-thought." She looked down at her paper and then agreed with me. "That's great," I encouraged, "Take the last ten minutes of this class period to improve your essay, add some sensory details and fix the last paragraph. With that, I'm sure your essay would pass on the writing test. We will look at it again tomorrow."

First lesson accomplished, I thought as I squeezed back behind my desk. The new method for teaching writing seemed to work. The bell rang and Amy said, "See you tomorrow, Ms. A."

"Yes, see you tomorrow." I answered and went to stand by my doorway to watch the students migrate to their next classes. I was pleased with the way this lesson went and felt like I was on the right track for teaching writing.

This process of tutoring for writing sounded easy, but sometimes it wasn't. Every student created a different writing scenario. Some were very creative, but used no periods to end sentences. Many students wrote one long paragraph instead of five. Basically, most students honestly believed that they could not write. They needed lots of encouragement.

One common problem was that students misread the test prompts. The three types of prompts were narrative, descriptive or persuasive essays. A student might write a perfectly comprehensive essay, but the essay did not persuade or describe or tell a story. That was a big reason for failing the test, not answering the prompt question correctly. Classroom teachers did not have the luxury of time to go through this writing process individually with 30 students in a classroom.

As a writing tutor, I could work with an individual student who was struggling with writing. I experienced great satisfaction whenever a student passed the Proficiency Writing Test and then came up in the writing center to personally thank me for my help. This teacher role was not half bad and much better than making a light bulb or serving a fancy drink at the race track. I was falling more and more in love with education.

Tutoring for the proficiency test was not my only new assignment from downstairs. I was put in charge of a brand new program called Senior Passports. I learned that "brand new" programs in education were very common and brand new teachers were often targeted for these brand new programs. Veteran teachers would look at the administrator and ask, "Are you crazy? You want me to do what? I don't have time for that!" So I became the Passport Advisor by default and probably because no other teacher would touch that job.

A passport was a glossy white folder containing three papers: an essay explaining a student's goals for the future, a second essay explaining their skills and a finished, polished résumé. Senior students were required to complete these three documents in their English classes, but if they didn't get them finished in class, they would be assigned to come to the writing center to finish them. The three documents were then printed on parchment paper.

Each 12th grade student had to complete their Senior Passport in order to graduate and it was up to me to make sure that they did. This shiny, white passport, a written and recorded bridge to the future, would be given to each senior along with their diploma at their graduation ceremony.

I was also in charge of storing and alphabetizing the finished passports. I checked passport folder names against a senior student list to be sure that every senior had completed this requirement. Passports were kept in large boxes inside the copy room of the English lounge where I spent hours alphabetizing and double checking the names.

Passport portfolios were a great idea, but not so much for students who didn't like to write, and that was a vast majority. Then getting the three papers written was like sailing a boat against the wind. We were getting nowhere fast. Luckily, at the end of the year when the brisk gale wind of the upcoming graduation started blowing, the seniors got busy writing.

Proficiency tutoring and passport portfolios kept the writing center all abuzz with activity, but I craved something more creative for my tutoring career to be complete. The answer came in the form of the annual Cuyahoga Falls Halloween Writing Contest. John, a 9th grade English teacher, had a room right across the hall from the writing center. He was a coach and his looks fit, a tall guy with sandy red hair, broad shoulders and a loud, booming voice. He loved intimidating the new freshmen with his gruff manner. One time I heard a commotion in his room and ran over to see if everything was okay. I found that John threw his shoe at the clock and knocked it off the wall because the bell rang to end class period before he was done with his lesson and the students wanted to leave.

My room was right across the hall from John's, so I often heard him bellowing at his students, and for this reason I was prepared to dislike him. But when I got to know him better, I found out John was a softie underneath that bluster and he really liked the kids more than they knew. Later I discovered that he was a Christian and made no bones about that fact. He often brought donuts and sometimes made homemade bread in his bread machine for the teachers on the third floor. My opinion of him soon reversed and he became one of my favorite English teachers. It was because of John that I found a creative venture for the writing center.

John told me about the Halloween Writing Contest offered in the Falls News Press and encouraged me to promote it. I was excited. I loved creative writing so got busy hanging contest flyers in the halls of the high school and in English classrooms. Then, I made sure the contest information was broadcast on the morning announcements. As a result, we received lots of entries of creative poems and stories from our students.

Creative writing was dear to me, so the writing contests didn't stop there. They expanded into Christmas and Valentine's Day. Promoting writing for fun produced extra work for me: planning the contests, designing flyers, advertising deadlines, soliciting prizes, appointing judges, printing out prize certificates and so on. But I didn't mind because I valued this creative side of writing and wanted to give students a chance to write creatively, not just write for a test.

Was the school year of 1998 to 1999 the best year in my life? Well, it was a year of discovery. If I wrote a recipe for my first year in the writing center, it would go something like this. Start with a pinch of kids who visited the writing center instead of going to the library or to study hall. Add in students who are assigned for proficiency tutoring in reading and writing. Mix well. Sprinkle in some seniors who must finish writing their Senior Passport Portfolios. Stir in books for lending and blend in writing contests complete with prizes. Pour onto the writing center tables and bake for 182 days until done or until summer vacation begins.

On the home front, my son Adam had a serious girlfriend, and they were making plans for a new future. He wasn't around very often between dating and working as a systems analyst at the Plain Dealer.

Earlene still lived in Pittsburgh with her family, Tom and their son Michael, my first grandson. Even though it was only a hundred miles away it seemed so distant. That was her home now, but I missed having her live close by.

Amber lived closer, in Ravenna, and was busy working at East Park Restaurant while taking care of her two daughters April and Melissa who were now in their teens. I cherished the time visiting with my family, especially my two granddaughters and my grandson in Pittsburgh.

My oldest son Earl lived in Freedom Township with his girlfriend. He scrounged scrap for extra money and worked doing various farm jobs like sorting corn or collecting sap to make maple syrup. He grew a huge garden and supplied the family with lots of sweet corn and fresh vegetables. During the summer months, Earl ran a produce stand and sold corn and vegetables at our little Kent Farmer's Market. He brought the freshest corn to the market because he got up early on Saturday, picked the corn by hand and threw it in the back of his old pickup truck. Then he drove straight to the market with the wet dew still clinging to the ears of corn. It hardly gets any fresher than that and it was delicious. He had a big following of regular customers. Because of Earl, our summer meals were the freshest tasting ever.

My two sons were totally opposite, one could drive a bus and fix my computer the other could clean my gutters and supply me with fresh picked produce.

Looking back at my Social Security statement, in the year 1997, my last year at General Electric, I made $36,000. The year I quit GE, did student teaching and started my new tutoring job at Cuyahoga Falls High School, 1998, I made $14,500, less than half from the year before. Seeing it in print, the dollar amount lost after quitting my good paying, secure job, you might wonder why I did that, but I knew why. My main goal for working in the past was to make money to live and support my family, but that had changed.

The satisfaction of teaching more than made up for the money. And hey, life is an adventure. At that time though, looking at my empty bank account, I realized I needed to find a job for the summer. My tutor pay did not extend over the summer months. Now since I was an official high school tutor, I thought this might qualify me for a part-time after school position at Sylvan Learning Center. It was time to update my résumé.

Job 16 – Sylvan Learning Center

Spring had not made an appearance yet as I drove out of the back parking lot of the high school on my way to interview for a position at Sylvan Learning Center in Cuyahoga Falls. I felt a little tired and down as I watched the snow hit my windshield in fat, wet splats. Maybe it was because for the first time in my life, I was living alone. My small house felt empty. True, I was living my dream of being a teacher but still needed a part time job for extra income. As usual, there was not a hint of romance in my life. Don't get all blue, I scolded myself. You have a lot to be thankful for and a decent job that you enjoy. I shook off the low feeling and pulled into the little plaza on Hudson Drive close by the entrance to Wal-Mart and Lowes.

I saw the sign that read, Sylvan Learning Center. These business centered educational facilities were springing up like new fast food restaurants. They were in every city. The state required that students pass the Ohio Proficiency Test in order to

180

graduate, so parents searched for extra help for their children. The Ohio standardized tests created a lot of anxiety. The administrators were worried because the school ratings were based on test results, which were published in the papers and tied to their school's funding. This worry trickled down to teachers, students and parents. Passing the test became big business. I wondered just how a learning center operated since it was a business. I was about to find out.

Best foot forward and wearing my boxy, dark interview suit, I entered the front door with my updated résumé in hand. The room was large and open. Groups of two or three students sat with a teacher at small square tables and worked on lessons. A pleasant looking woman with dark rimmed glasses, mid-length chestnut hair and an attractive, bookish appearance greeted me and introduced herself as Pam. She looked like a librarian, but her friendly demeanor put me at ease right away.

Pam explained how Sylvan worked and the duties of a tutor. Each student who enrolled at Sylvan was tested to find their weakest academic area and from that Sylvan could determine which lessons they would need to work on for improvement. For instance, if the student tested weak in vocabulary, their lessons were geared toward learning new vocabulary. This could be especially helpful to kids planning on taking SAT tests for college. It was the same for math, grammar, reading and so on.

20 Jobs: A Memoir

Sylvan was a business, corporate funded and franchised, that had started in 1979 at the Sylvan Hill Medical Center Building in Portland, Oregon. There they developed a business plan for their tutoring program. Maybe that explained their success, a solid business plan. Comparing Sylvan's way to our high school, I realized that when students started 9th grade, teachers usually had no idea of each student's capabilities, strengths or weaknesses. Why? I wondered. Maybe we needed a business plan or regular pre-testing at the high school or junior high school.

Pam was impressed with my credentials as a writing center coordinator. They were ideal for this type of work since I was already a tutor. That made it easy to get hired, or maybe it was easy because the pay wasn't a whole lot and the hours were erratic and short, mostly after school hours. I could probably earn more money as a waitress but was not going back to that era in my life. I wanted to work in education. The short hours fit my schedule because I didn't want a second job that took up a lot of my extra time.

My evenings were already filling up pretty quickly. One night a week, I practiced with the church singing choir and church bell choir. In addition, I continued to volunteer on the weekends as a tour guide at Stan Hywet Hall and Gardens in Akron. The tour guide position started out as an extracurricular activity to jazz up my résumé, but I stayed there because I loved the historic atmosphere of the Tudor style house and the beauty of the English and Japanese gardens. I enjoyed learning the history of the Seiberling family and had fun ushering people through the mansion. Though I no longer worked evenings on a second shift job, I still spent many evenings doing extra activities, paid and non-paid.

Working at Sylvan's added more driving to my day, mostly because of Shorty. After the day ended, I dashed the five miles home through traffic, let my poor, old dog Shorty out for a potty break, grabbed a quick snack, and headed back to Sylvan Learning Center. I felt like a pendulum, coming and going back and forth between jobs, home and church activities.

Shorty was an unexpected present from my daughter Amber when she moved into a trailer park that didn't allow dogs. He was short, hence the name, and had big sad, brown eyes. Shorty also shed hair by the bushels and ran away whenever you turned your back. My two granddaughters, April and Melissa loved him. When they moved, Shorty either had to go to grandma's house or to the dog pound. I couldn't let Shorty go to the pound and break my granddaughters' hearts, so that's how Shorty came to live with me. Add dog duties to the other run around chores of a single mom, or single woman, since Adam no longer lived at home, and it was a turnstile existence of coming and going. I was working more hours than I did at GE and making less money. Well, I chose this new education path and was walking it the best way I knew how.

20 Jobs: A Memoir

One benefit about being a Sylvan tutor was that once I sat down at the table, the learning plan or curriculum was done. Sylvan teachers just presented and followed through with the lessons for each student. No prep work! After they completed their lesson assignments and a short quiz, I checked off each task on the student's predetermined learning plan. It was efficient to the point of boring. If a student had homework, I could help them with that since Sylvan offered homework help. Either way, I sat by a student as he or she worked diligently on lessons and watched the clock crawl along, reminiscent of GE time. I fought the boredom and reminded myself that tutoring was more rewarding than just making light bulbs - that helped. After working at the high school all day and then at Sylvan, I was mentally exhausted, different than being physically exhausted after a day at GE.

Most students did not come through the front door of Sylvan wearing happy faces. I could tell that they were tired of sitting in school when they arrived to face even more sitting and more lessons. Most likely they were ready for some physical activity and probably hungry since young stomachs are always empty. But here they were, straight from school and on to Sylvan - back at the books.

The majority of our Sylvan students were not failing academically. Even though they were a little weak in one subject, most of them were getting passing grades in school. The parents, who were upper-middle class, wanted their children to achieve the best possible grades and get into a prestigious college and then into a high-paying profession. Students were at Sylvan because their parents wanted them to achieve academic success in order to have a secure future. Realizing that after-school-tutoring was not often pleasant for our students, I tried to add some humor and lightness to their afternoon. I talked to them about their outside activities or asked them what they were reading in school or reading for fun. I made little jokes to lighten their mood. Sometimes it worked and sometimes not.

One day when I arrived at Sylvan, I noticed a curious book tucked under the arm of one of my students, an 8th grade boy. On the book cover was a peculiar looking dark-haired boy in round glasses riding on a broom and the name on the cover was Harry Potter. What a bizarre picture and title, I thought. We sat down at our table, and as soon as I mentioned the book, his face brightened up. He became animated and excited as he told me about this boy wizard and Hogwarts School. Judging from my student's lively reaction, I decided that I had better read that book. This was a time when not many readers had yet discovered Harry Potter except for a select, few middle school kids. I bought Harry Potter, read it and loved it.

A book like this needed to be shared and I found the perfect person at the high school, Kathy, who was an attendant for a handicapped student in a wheelchair. Kathy had short, straight red-auburn hair and a can-do personality. She often offered to help teachers in their classes or run extra errands. I can't remember a day when she didn't have a positive attitude. She enjoyed the kids and brightened their day with her smile and laughter. Best of all for me, we both enjoyed reading and discussing books.

Kathy visited with me in the writing center every day on her way through to the teacher's lounge. When I discovered how much Kathy loved to read, we started recommending and sharing books together. We formed a bond as ardent fans of Harry Potter and it became our mission to get more students and teachers to read it. To this day we argue whether I read Harry Potter first and got her to read it or vice versa. Either way, we both read it and loved it. I can remember begging other teachers to give the book a chance. Just read it, I would say. It's dumb or childish, they would answer. We don't like books about magic, witchcraft or sorcery.

Eventually, with extra urging, some teachers read Harry Potter and became as excited about it as we were. There was only one book out at the time, *Harry Potter and the Sorcerer's Stone,* but Kathy and I were anxiously waiting for the next year at Hogwarts to begin. It's ironic, but at first I didn't even realize that J.K. Rowling was a woman. Men usually wrote Fantasy or Science Fiction. Our passion for the Harry Potter saga continued for eight more years. I often wanted to thank that 8th grade student at Sylvan for this magical discovery . . . or was it Kathy?

Kathy and I shared another bond besides reading. On September 11, 2001, she came running into the writing center and said, "Quick, turn on the radio. Something terrible just happened in New York City."

It was the beginning of the school day and students were in their first period classes. There were no TV's and not many radios in the school. Thinking it couldn't be that serious, but to appease Kathy, I turned on my radio and tried to find the news. Nothing! Then we remembered that one of my Powermac computers could access TV. I'm sure one of the students had shown me this cool feature. We turned on the Powermac and got a TV station to show up in a tiny, fuzzy black and white square.

An anxious voice reported that a plane had smashed into one of the Twin Towers in New York City. Oh dear God, this was serious. What was happening? Was it an accident? Kathy and I hunched shoulder to shoulder over the tiny screen and watched the burning tower when suddenly we saw a second plane come into view, circle around and fly into the second Twin Tower. We both gasped in disbelief. This was definitely not an accident! It wasn't long before other teachers and students gathered by us in a knot around the tiny computer screen. Everyone was stunned into silence as we watched people jump to their deaths from the burning buildings and eventually saw the towers fall in a cloud of dust like an upside down atomic bomb. Unbelievable!

The news kept getting worse as we heard that the Pentagon was hit by a plane and more people were killed The main office put out an announcement that students were allowed to leave if a parent picked them up. Word spread and students were crying and crowding together in tight knots in the halls between classes. School had to continue since a lot of parents worked and nobody was at home. Our students were better off being with their friends at school while they digested the horrible news of the attack on our country. I wanted to be with my family, but was glad to have Kathy by my side during this time. I will always remember that morning and can't hear the words 9/11 without thinking of Kathy and Cuyahoga Falls High School.

Working at Sylvan along with the high school was giving me just enough extra income to get by, but when it was getting close to summer break, I knew that it was time to find some full time work for the summer. My tutoring pay at the high school did not carry over to June, July and August and there was not much summer work at Sylvan. I couldn't live three months without a paycheck, especially after my huge drop in income. Now with a teaching license, there should be more opportunities open for me. I thought about teaching summer school, but it was too late to apply. Since I was lucky in jobs, but not in love, the answer came from an ad in the local paper. *Secretary needed for Camp Asbury in Hiram.* Time to tune up the résumé and this time stress my computer skills for working in an office.

Job 17 - Camp Asbury

I called the number from the ad and was now on my way for an interview as an office secretary at Camp Asbury, which was located in Hiram on Asbury Road, about 15 miles from my home in Kent. The country roads were familiar, in fact I was about to drive right past my old farm house in Freedom, the happy place where I raised my four kids and the sorrowful place where I lost everything during my divorce. As I approached the house, I automatically slowed down and my hands clenched on the steering wheel of the 1990 Honda Civic Hatchback. Keep going, I told myself, don't look back - too many memories in that house. I kept my eyes straight and stepped on the gas.

When I worked at General Electric, I had leased a newer car since I could afford a car payment. The lease had run out and my pay was cut in half, so I saved money by inheriting my son Adam's old car. He had a decent job at the Plain Dealer and bought a newer Honda to drive to Cleveland. He donated his old blue Honda to a worthy cause . . . me. The car ran like a top and was great on gas mileage with only one minor problem, the air conditioner was broken. That didn't bother me. I had driven many clunkers in my life and knew that under the hood, this little Honda was a dependable running car, so the air conditioner was the least of my worries. I just carried a spray bottle of water as a redneck cooling system for the hottest days. On my way to the interview, the windows were rolled up to keep my hair from blowing into a tangled mess.

Down State Route 303, left on Asbury Road and a few miles more around some curvy bends and then up the hill, I spotted the wooden sign for Camp Asbury and pulled off onto a dirt parking lot on the right. A rustic wood-framed building sat up on a small slope next to the parking lot. That had to be the office I decided as I shifted into reverse, the parking gear for a stick shift. I turned off the engine, got out and walked up to the door.

The door was open, so I walked in and was greeted by the director of the camp, William. He was a nice looking man with a thin face, dark eyes, brown hair and a full sandy, brown mustache that nicely accentuated his face. He resembled a world explorer in his brown khaki shorts and shirt. The front office was small with a desk and chair sitting in front of the window. On the other side of the room sat a large cage containing a furry critter that I later learned was a chinchilla named Oreo.

20 Jobs: A Memoir

Bill, as he asked me to call him, was very pleasant and explained that he was new as director of the camp and was still learning about his camp duties. We chatted more and I made it clear right up front that I could only work during the summer since I'd be going back to teaching at the high school in the fall. Bill answered that this was perfectly fine since Camp Asbury had programs for day camps and week-long camps during the summer and this was their busiest time of the year. He seemed to like my credentials and hired me as the summer secretary for Camp Asbury.

I was pleased to get this position, but not overjoyed like when I got the job at GE or when I stepped into my first teaching position, probably because I knew this was a temporary position. I didn't know it yet, but like many new ventures or job beginnings, working at a summer camp would ultimately provide added skills, different perspectives and new friends who would influence my future in unexpected ways.

As it turned out, Bill was a minister and Asbury was a United Methodist camp. I soon realized that Camp Asbury was a 450 acre year-round camp and retreat center. The camp featured canoeing, hiking, swimming, high and low challenge courses, star gazing and a giant mudslide. It was a fun place to work.

At first, being camp secretary was a little like working for my sister Jane because I didn't know exactly what it involved. But as the summer got into full swing, I found my way. After so many changes in my life, I adapted quickly. I learned how to file and how to keep track of camp activities, camp schedules and employee records. Along with that, a big part of camp life was communication, answering the phone and passing messages from the office staff to camp counselors and other workers. The office duties kept me busy and my boss Bill was always pleasant.

That summer, spending my days at Camp Asbury, I came to be conscious of how much I missed the country and rhythm of nature as part of my life. It brought back fond memories of living in Freedom on our small farm. Some days as I drove to work down the back roads, I saw deer or wild raccoons frolicking with their babies in the middle of the road. At camp when I walked the short distance back to the dining lodge soaking up the sun and smells of fresh country air, I felt at peace. The office was surrounded by a lake and rolling hills, such a lovely setting. It restored my spirit to be out in nature more. Even though I now lived in town, I was forever a country girl at heart.

Working in the office, I had the chance to get acquainted with the camp workers and counselors. Who knew that out here in the small camp I would meet young people from South Africa, Poland, Germany and Russia? They came from various parts of the world to work at Camp Asbury and learn about America and its culture. One of their main objectives was to become more fluent in English.

English is essential because it is the business language, so men and women from around the world sought the experience of living for a brief time in America to learn English while getting paid. As the secretary, I knew counselors didn't make much money; therefore, their main advantage was the exposure to our culture and language. Along with the beauty of spending the summer in the country, this job gave me the chance to broaden my perspective and learn about different cultures.

I became friends with Natalie from Russia and Magda from Poland. Natalie was quiet and very pretty with dark eyes and dark hair. She had a gentle, amiable nature and often brought me little bouquets of wild flowers that I displayed in a tiny teapot on my desk. I smile whenever I think of Natalie and remember her sweet nature and kind gestures. I learned from Natalie that life in Russia was complicated and that the medical care in her country was woefully lacking compared to medical care in America.

Magda, the kitchen assistant, was different from Natalie but also kind and soft spoken. She was lovely and willowy thin with shoulder length, straight blonde hair. Magda had a serious outlook and strong opinions, especially concerning her work as assistant camp cook.

Some of the main foods at that time at Camp were prepackaged chicken nuggets, hamburgers, corn dogs, pizza and macaroni and cheese - the typical American diet for young people. Magda was indignant and could not believe what kind of food we served our campers. In Poland she cooked fresh food from scratch, and often went on and on about this horrible camp menu. Magda was emotional about other things that she felt were not right in America. I would listen to her and nod my head in agreement.

Working in the office, I arranged for Magda to phone home to Poland or receive phone calls back from her family. Cell phones were not common and she was extremely homesick for communication with her husband and two children. I felt empathy for her situation and wanted to help her contact her family whenever I could.

Magda also had a bold side and wanted to experience as much of America as possible in one short summer. I admired her adventuresome spirit and we would often visit other places away from camp. We drove together in my old Honda and traveled to Sea World and Stan Hywet Hall and Gardens.

At Sea World, Magda and I visited all the attractions and then went to see Shamu, Sea World's famous killer whale. Magda wanted to sit up front in the splash zone. I reluctantly followed her down to the front bleachers, but wasn't looking forward to getting wet. But for Magda, I would sit there. As expected, when Shamu hit the water with his big whale tail we were soaked clear through. The sun set and we were shivering as we made our way back to the car. On the drive back to camp, Magda said she didn't care if we were cold and wet because it was an honor to be splashed by such a fantastic whale. I had to agree as I turned up the heater in the Honda, which fortunately did work.

When we visited Stan Hywet Hall and Gardens, Magda admired the Tudor style house and beautiful Japanese and English gardens. We walked through the birch tree alley and came out upon a wedding party being photographed on the famous west balcony that overlooked the Cuyahoga Valley National Park. Without hesitation, Magda walked right over and joined the bride and groom who were posing on the balcony for pictures and asked me to take her picture with them. I was a little embarrassed, and hastily explained that Magda was visiting from Poland as I pulled out my camera. The bride and groom were gracious and pleased to share their happiness with a visitor from another country. Magda did not want to miss any part of American life and I loved seeing America through her eyes, the good and the bad.

Greg was another counselor from Poland. He was handsome and athletic, with blond hair. As the youth counselor for Bike Camp, Greg would ride his bike 40 or 50 miles on a weekend to explore places around the area. He rode from Camp Asbury clear down to the Cuyahoga Valley National Park. I warned him to be careful about traffic and worried about his safety knowing how motorists had no respect for bicyclists on American highways. This fact didn't bother Greg. He rode right next to the traffic and went wherever he wanted to go by bicycle.

G.H. Ashenfelter

I really admired both Greg and Magda. My dad was Polish and my grandfather came from Warsaw, Poland, so I felt connected to them by my European heritage.

At camp, we had a Gator. Not a live alligator, but an open jeep type vehicle that could go over different types of terrain, very handy in case of an emergency at a distant part of the campgrounds. We had such an emergency one time when a big tree branch fell on a hiker. Luckily, the girl was only frightened, and not seriously injured. Bill was there in flash with the Gator. We needed up-to-date communication methods, so we also had walkie-talkies to keep in contact with campers in the woods. Safety measures were a priority at the camp.

Greg loved driving the Gator almost as much as he loved riding his bike. One day Greg invited me to join him and ride out in the open Gator to see the new ropes course. I had never heard of a ropes course before, so was anxious to go and observe our counselors in action. Bill nodded his approval for me to take a break from the office. I felt a little like Safari Jane as I climbed into the open Gator and hung on tight. We bounced down the pathway into the woods and out to where the campers were preparing to fly through the trees attached to a zip line.

I stepped out of the Gator and watched as our counselor Rachel helped a pre-teen girl into a harness and then attached her harness to the rope line with a carabineer, a metal ring with a spring hinged side used as a connector to hold a freely running rope. Rachel held the rope and encouraged the camper not to be afraid. The girl hesitantly climbed up onto a high platform, paused, then suddenly she stepped forward, and whoosh, she flew down the zip line through the trees toward another counselor who was waiting to catch her. My heart did a little flip flop. How safe was this line that was strung high through the trees? I found out that it was super safe and fortunately, the camp counselors knew what they were doing and kept all our campers free from injury. What a great way to build confidence in young people! I was getting to know a lot more of camp life and enjoyed the adventure of riding in the Gator.

Bill came up with the enterprising idea of opening a camp store to sell shirts and hats featuring a Camp Asbury Logo. A circle with a cross in the middle and the name Camp Asbury written below became the camp insignia. Shirts, hats and assorted memorabilia were ordered to stock the store. It was the ideal place for parents to buy camp merchandise for their kids to remember their experiences at camp. A small one-room building by the parking lot was easily transformed into a store to stock our new merchandise. I became the new store manager and clerk all in one. It was a task that I enjoyed and my only taste of retail work.

Because of this little store, my work uniform for the summer became a khaki Camp Asbury shirt, light colored Dockers and sometimes a cloth bucket hat. That suited me just fine because I was never a fan of dressing up in formal clothes. Since the store was part of my office duties, I stayed late on Friday afternoons. After each week-long camp, the campers, their families, the camp counselors and other camp staff would gather on the hillside overlooking the peaceful lake for a closing ceremony of songs and prayers. I often walked across the rolling lawns to observe this ritual. The campers sang songs and acted out skits they had learned to entertain their parents. After that, I hurried back by the office and opened the store to sell souvenirs to the departing families, tokens and mementos of the adventures that the kids had experienced at camp.

My position as secretary at Camp Asbury gave me just enough money to live on that summer, but not much to spare. I was slick about inviting myself to dinner at various places and this shameless audacity served me well that summer. It just so happened that each day after camp, I had to drive right by my brother Joe and sister-in-law Michelle's house around suppertime. I would conveniently stop by to say hello and Michelle always invited me to stay for dinner. Nice! My plan worked! Michelle prepared a delicious home-cooked meal each night for Joe, and now for me too.

After awhile, they expected me to show up at dinner time, which I usually did. I could never count how many meals they fed me throughout the years, but let's just say "numerous meals." Michelle and I were always close and she was like another daughter to me. She never once complained about her constant summer dinner-time guest. On the other hand, my brother Joe kept asking for my Social Security number so he could claim me on his taxes.

Joe and Michelle had another summer guest. A mama groundhog was hit on the road in front of their house leaving behind an orphaned baby groundhog. At various times, Joe and Michelle had raised baby deer, a baby fox, and assorted other wild life, so they readily adopted the baby groundhog and it lived in a cage in their living room. He was so cute. Being a baby, the ground hog imprinted on Michelle right away. He waddled around on his short baby legs and followed her everywhere. They named him Chuckie.

Evenings when I stopped by for dinner, I would hold Chuckie tenderly and feed him a bottle. Then he would cuddle up on my neck and go to sleep. I was extremely attached to the little rodent. He was growing up into a fine looking little groundhog, but then a terrible mistake happened. Accidently, they fed him Cocoa Puffs cereal not thinking about the results of chocolate on wild animals. Our poor little Chuckie groundhog became extremely ill and eventually died. I know it sounds silly to be emotional about a groundhog, but I was. Whenever I think of my first summer at Camp Asbury, I remember that tiny groundhog and still miss him.

G.H. Ashenfelter

I returned to teaching at Cuyahoga Falls at the end of August and made plans to be camp secretary the following summer. And I did return to Camp Asbury, but things were different from my first summer. Bill had hired a new full-time secretary and I didn't care for her much. She was friendly enough, but very possessive about the office duties and the files. She made it clear that she was the top secretary and even occupied my desk by the window.

I now spent most of my time running errands or working in the store. Yes, things had changed for me around Camp Asbury. I no longer felt needed. I knew that I would not be returning to camp the next summer and would seek another way to supplement my income. I finished out the second summer running the store and doing other odd jobs, but I was no longer the real camp secretary. Greg returned to camp that second year, but Magda did not. It felt different without her. Fortunately, I remained in touch with Magda through mail and email.

∞∞∞∞∞∞∞∞∞∞

As it turned out, in 2009, thanks to Magda and my niece Heather, I visited Warsaw, the city of my grandfather Julius, my dad's father. This visit to Poland was in part due to my continued friendship with Magda and in part due to the fact that my niece Heather lived in Germany. My dear high school friend Jan and I made the trip to Germany first to visit Heather and then we took the train to Poland.

Magda had agreed to meet with us on the train in Berlin and travel on with us to Warsaw where she took on the role of our personal tour guide and Polish translator. Leaving from Berlin, Heather, Jan and I were seated on the train in a six seat compartment just like in the Hogwarts train in the Harry Potter movies. Suddenly Magda appeared outside the compartment window. She found us and it was wonderful to see her after so many years. She looked just the same, lovely as ever and willowy thin with straight blonde hair down to her shoulders.

We traveled on together to Warsaw and stayed at an apartment in what was once part of the Jewish "Ghetto." Magda had borrowed the apartment from a friend who was out of town, so we did not have to pay hotel bills.

The first day in Warsaw, we visited the Warsaw Rising Museum and learned the history of the city during the war. The museum chronicled the story of the brave Poles; men, women and children who tried in vain to save their city from the German invasion. This was a horrific time in Polish history. During WWII, in 1944, between August and October, Poles fought valiantly against the Nazis. Most of the city was completely destroyed. I felt overcome with sadness at the museum as I remembered that Warsaw was the birth city of my grandfather and Heather's great grandfather, Julius, who had immigrated to America in 1910. His parents remained in Warsaw and I wondered if any of our relatives took part in that battle. Jan also had ancestors from Poland so it was a meaningful trip for all of us.

We spent two days in Warsaw and then traveled north by train to stay with Magda and her family in their home in Chojna in eastern Poland. We had the pleasure of meeting Magda's husband, son, daughter and father. Her mother had recently passed and we visited the little church graveyard where she was laid to rest. It was a trip I will always remember and cherish.

Magda and her family made us feel welcome and I was even more proud of my Polish heritage. I am eternally grateful for her friendship and therefore grateful for my job at Camp Asbury. That seemingly insignificant secretary position gave me the chance to learn about camp life and meet a wide variety of people. It also enabled me to walk where my grandfather once walked, Warsaw, Poland.

∞∞∞∞∞∞∞∞∞∞

Sadly, my dad passed away before I visited Poland. He fought a valiant fight against lung cancer and died in March of 2003. Dad was against going to a nursing home. "He didn't want to be with all those 'old' people," he said. With help from hospice, my younger sister Jane and her husband Ray took care of him in their home. Dad was content to live out his last days there and I will be forever grateful to Jane and Ray for their loving care of our dad. They handled his illness and care with grace and humor and made sure his last days were comfortable and dignified. I was sorry that I never had the chance to tell him about our trip to Poland. He would have been so pleased to know that Heather and I visited Warsaw, the home of his father.

Job 18 - Summer School

Back in my third year at Cuyahoga Falls High School, again, the writing center position was my only job option. In spite of numerous interviews that summer, I was not hired as a classroom teacher. Going into teaching, I fully expected to be in a regular classroom position without needing to work a second job. Still I continued to work as an ISGI tutor in the writing center. No matter how many interviews, I couldn't seem to get a classroom teaching position.

Other English teachers consoled me with tales of how well qualified teachers were often passed over in favor of coaches or other less qualified teachers who had more connections. They assured me that I was well qualified, but it was school politics. I convinced myself that this might be true, but in the back of my mind I thought, maybe they think I'm too old. It was discouraging that I couldn't get a position in a regular classroom instead of remaining as a tutor in the writing center.

The first day after summer break, students were directed on the PA system to go directly to their new homerooms before 1st period. My little room with the round, brown tables sat empty. Some of last year's writing center students, Barry, Tom, Rob,

Sarah, and Ryan, poked their heads in the doorway and yelled, "Hi, Ms. A." That lightened my mood as I waved back a cheery hello.

It didn't take long before the writing center was back in full swing. As the year progressed, more students used my little room and it continued to grow, as least in the number of students though not in size. It was a challenge to start a book club and recruit students who liked to read. The book club students had fun as they did fundraisers in order to buy our books. They sold hot dogs in front of the Acme store and gift wrapped books at Borders Book Store before Christmas. I knew the book club was a true success when we finally had a group picture taken for the year book. In addition, this year was the first for an anthology magazine that featured stories and poetry written by our students. It turned out to be a huge hit. So the writing center buzzed along with new activities and was now my home away from home.

As the end of the school year approached, I applied for any open summer school English teaching position. I would not return to Camp Asbury. That chapter was closed. Pam at Sylvan Learning Center offered me an open position to tutor one evening a week. That could help some with the money, but it was not enough, so I turned her down. But not working and therefore having no paycheck in the summer was an option I could scarcely afford.

Luckily, job-seeking fortune shined down on me, as usual, and I was hired to teach 9th and 10th grade English summer school at Central School in

Kent, which was about a mile from my house. It fit the bill! A summer teaching position would give me the chance to prove myself in a real classroom situation and after that, I was sure to be hired as a classroom teacher at Cuyahoga Falls. This teaching experience would look perfect on my résumé for the upcoming fall school year.

As soon as the semester came to a close, I drove over to Central School to prepare my new classroom. With no prior summer school experience, I didn't know what to expect when I walked into the long rectangular brick building. After the bustle of our high school, it was surprising how empty a school felt without students. I located an office worker who directed me to a room right down the hall from the main office. When I walked into that classroom, I caught my breath. It was the room I had pictured in my head the day I started at Cuyahoga Falls. Immediately, I felt at home. It was spacious with real student desks and a polished, wooden teacher's desk in the front of the room. Dappled sunlight streamed in through large windows that overlooked green trees and a lawn. It was totally different from my little narrow inside room at Cuyahoga Falls. It was my classroom over the rainbow.

To start, I searched for books and maybe a curriculum to use in my class. I was concerned when I found out that there was no specific curriculum to follow. Most teachers already had a curriculum they used, but since I was not a regular classroom teacher, I did not. There were class sets of books stored in a back room that I could use, which had stories with written assignments, but no specific lessons. I was on my own with that. In our English lounge, I dug up a daily grammar exercise workbook and some stray English text books. Then I went to work preparing lessons.

If I remember correctly, summer school was in session four days a week for eight or nine weeks, Monday through Thursday. The hours were from 8:00 a.m. to 12:00 noon, a long block of time to fill up with just one subject. It would require intense preparation to keep the class work interesting and the students engaged for this length of time, especially since I didn't carry year-long lesson plans in my back pocket. This was going to be a challenge.

The first day in my summer classroom, I greeted each of my nineteen students at the door and acted very casual and friendly, trying not to show my trepidation. I didn't want them to know this was my first time on my own as a classroom teacher. I was comfortable around teens from tutoring at the high school and truly liked the age group, so they picked up on that.

The class was made up of a mix of girls and boys, but more boys, since English was usually not the best subject for boys. Looking around the room when everyone was seated, I noticed that the students were more racially diverse than students from Cuyahoga Falls. Introducing myself, I didn't mention that I was a lowly writing center teacher. As far as they knew, I had been teaching in a classroom all my life and was old enough to look the part. The show was on.

On that first day, we did some get acquainted exercises and then some silent reading to fill up time. The nicest part about a three hour class was that students could finish their work in the classroom, so I didn't assign any homework. The worst part was that I had to come up with enough lessons each day to fill up those three hours.

Lesson preparation kept me busy and the weeks flew by. At times students were a little suspicious of me and said that I didn't act like most teachers. I wasn't sure if that was a compliment or a sign that they were on to my "teaching forever" disguise. I prepared and taught what I liked best, lots of poetry, literature and open discussion with a smidgeon of grammar. We studied Martin Luther King Jr. and other stories from the Civil Rights Era. We made poetry books and watched movies. This was my first real classroom and I looked forward to being there each morning, pleased that the students seemed to enjoy my class where the atmosphere was free and easy like a summer breeze.

We settled into the summer schedule with no discipline problems. I'd like to say my winning personality won the students over - at least that was a theory. Whatever had happened, the students got along well and had fun during our class. Learning should be fun, right? Truly, they were a great group of teens and I was an eager beaver teacher who did my best to make my first real lessons interesting and diverse. It just worked out.

There were no other summer classes in the building, but once a day we had a visitor. A stout lady with a round face and sunny smile would pass by in our hallway and peek around the corner of the door into my classroom to say hello. Our class would greet her heartily with smiles and waves every time she appeared. She worked in an office at the end of the hall, but I was not sure what she did in that office.

Later I learned that her name was Joyce and during breaks we would often meet in the hall to chat. It came to light that she worked for the Sixth District Compact for Kent City Schools and wrote grants for their GED programs. Joyce complimented me on how lively and cheerful my classroom was when she walked by. I told her I always made my classroom fun and interactive, but then confessed that I was not what I seemed. I was just a beginning teacher and this was my first real class. Even though I was in my 50s, I was not burned out from teaching for years in the classroom. Summer school was a new exciting adventure for me and I loved it. Joyce laughed and agreed to keep my true identity a secret from the kids.

∞∞∞∞∞∞∞∞∞

In downtown Kent along the Riveredge Trail, there is a wooden plaque commemorating the historical site where Captain Samuel Brady supposedly jumped 21 feet across the Cuyahoga River to avoid a band of Indians in 1780. I was shocked that my summer school students were not aware of this amazing death-defying feat even though most of them lived in Kent. I decided that we should brush up on local history by going on a field trip, but then wondered if summer school students were allowed to take field trips.

Our class deserved a break away from the indoor classroom and maybe we could take a walking field trip. I inquired about this and after filling out the numerous forms, the trip was approved by the high school principal. Since Central School was very close to downtown Kent, we could just walk a few blocks to our historic destination. To connect this trip to more educational and historical facts about Kent, we would start out by exploring the small museum that was located upstairs above the Pufferbelly Restaurant and then continue on with a walk along the Riveredge Trail to end up at the famous Brady's Leap Memorial plaque.

It was a perfect summer day for a field trip. The sun cast moving shadows through the leaves onto the sidewalks and the air was filled with the smell of freshly mowed lawns. We were in high spirits as we walked towards town - me in the lead. I was vaguely aware of how odd we must look; a middle aged woman leading nineteen gangly teens, most of them a head taller than me, down the Main Street of Kent. I noticed that some drivers turned and gawked. Did they wonder what we were doing or who we were? I acted like a mother hen with her over-grown chicks as I often turned around and looked back to make sure they were safely behind me. At first I felt self-conscious, but then thought, who cares? This is exactly where I want to be today, with my class on a field trip. The kids didn't notice or care who was watching as they talked and laughed, enjoying their freedom from the stuffy classroom.

Arriving at the Pufferbelly, we traipsed in a single line up the narrow stairs to the museum. There we gaped at old remnants of town history that peered back from another era at our reflections in the glass cases; old sepia photos of early Kent settlers and remnants of their lives, so different from our modern lives. In a short time, the students were more interested in visiting with each other than looking at historic mementoes, so we exited the museum to begin our walk along the river.

Many of my students, even those who lived in Kent, had never been on the Riveredge Trail and were amazed that it ran right through the middle of town hidden from view below the Main Street bridge. We located the steep wooden stairs that were tucked away in the back of the law office parking lot and descended down to the path that followed along the Cuyahoga River. On the path, the students eagerly explored the scenic views from newly constructed wooden lookouts. We stopped and gazed down at the waterfall or admired the swirling waters of the Cuyahoga River.

When we reached Brady's Leap, I asked a student to read the story on the plaque out loud and we listened politely. When he finished, we all marveled that in 1780 Captain Brady jumped 21 feet across the river to escape his death. But ultimately, we decided that if Indians were chasing us, we could do it too.

Happily, I didn't lose even one student on the field trip. After that day, the students constantly asked for another field trip. They didn't care where. Unfortunately, Kent was not going to supply a bus to transport a summer school class, and there were no other points of interest to explore in Kent unless it was the college hang-out, Ray's Bar and Grill. We were not going there!

My first summer school class ended on a high note and it was a time that I will always remember because it was my very first actual English classroom. I think that some magic mingled with learning that summer, at least it did in my memory. Whenever I take a walk by the Cuyahoga River, I picture the faces of my first official students and hear their happy teen voices. Our class bonded and formed a positive learning community that summer. My experiences with those 9th and 10th grade students gave me the confidence to believe that I could be a successful teacher, not just a tutor, if I was ever given the chance.

∞∞∞∞∞∞∞∞∞∞∞

In the fall, buoyed up from my rewarding summer school at Central School, I applied for numerous English classroom positions, only to be passed over for "more qualified" teachers. Sigh! It was frustrating. Fortunately this new school year in the writing center offered some improvements in my status quo. I was assigned a different room on the second floor with even more computers. It was two or three times larger than my tiny third floor room with one less flight of steps to climb each day.

Best of all, the room had large windows on the west side. Keep in mind that I spent thirteen years at General Electric on second shift with no view of the outside world, just machines and noise, windows meant a great deal to me. It was delightful to watch the trees change each season, grow leaves and then drop them down against the background of the ever changing color of the sky. I was a poet and dreamer at heart when it came to watching nature.

With my new roomy classroom, I could accommodate more students for writing assignments. This changed the dynamics of the writing center. Teachers now came in with their classes to complete assignments on the computers. When the students were writing or searching for information, if they didn't need any immediate help, I chatted with the teachers. This helped me become better acquainted with more students and teachers and better informed on school news and activities. The English teachers began accepting me as one of their own and not just a tutor. The writing center was evolving even more.

After my time at Central School, I was optimistic about seeking summer school employment again. The next spring, I applied for a summer school position as soon as the jobs were posted. Reality often changes and I realized that was true when I was assigned to teach 12th grade summer school at Roosevelt High School, not 9th and 10th at Central School. This should be an interesting summer, I mused.

As soon as our spring semester ended, I went up to Kent High School to find my room and hopefully some curriculum materials. But again I faced the same problem as at Central School, no set curriculum. I sought out other teachers at the high school and asked if there was a curriculum I could use to teach 12th grade English. Well, no, not really, they answered. Some teachers tried to be helpful and showed me where to search school storage areas to find books for that grade level. Like last summer, I was on my own with the class content.

Since I was teaching 12th grade, I was sure students had some requirements to meet to graduate, but basically the requirements seemed to be an earned credit for English taught by any qualified teacher they could rope into teaching during the summer months, like me. Veteran teachers were usually not interested in teaching summer school. They had bigger salaries and did not need the extra work.

My new class consisted of twelve seniors, 17 or 18 years old, who were not thrilled about losing part of their summer to earn an English credit, but they needed the credit to graduate. Right away I noticed that this group was not as friendly and open as my 9th and 10th graders were last summer. This group was more mature and ready to be done with school. I wasn't so sure I could fool them with the

"I've been teaching for years" disguise. But I decided to try.

Teaching twelfth grade was more of a challenge. One of my new students, a girl named Amy, angrily demanded to know why I wasn't teaching British Literature. She planned to go to college and needed that subject. Good question, I thought, knowing that I didn't have the books or background experience to teach that class. I could have asked her why she didn't pass it in the first place, but decided against that. Another senior, Brittany who was a cosmetology student constantly did her nails or browsed fashion magazines. She didn't care what I taught. And then there was James who kept his head down most of the time and slept.

"You have to keep awake in class," I urged James.

"I can't keep awake," he answered hoarsely as he barely raised his head. "I work most of the night and don't get any sleep."

"Well, at least try." I said. What else could I say? I knew James wanted to graduate. He tried to keep up with our work and participated as much as possible. I admired his honesty.

When I relied on movies to fill the long hours in class, James would catch up on his sleep. Was I too easy on these kids? I didn't really want to fail them and stop them from graduating, so decided to work with them the best I could. Brittany, who was all about the glamour and becoming a beautician; Kathy, who was a little overweight, withdrawn and would never turn in her papers; Amy who wanted

G.H. Ashenfelter

British Literature; James, who couldn't stay awake. Each one needed this English credit to graduate. But then there was Thomas.

Thomas was witty and smart with an Ivy League, clean-cut look and friendly open smile. I liked him right away and could easily picture him walking down the halls of an exclusive college like Harvard. Why had he ended up in a summer school class? Judging from his quick wit and confident demeanor, I thought he could probably teach the class. When Thomas handed in his first paper, I noticed that he forgot to put his name at the top. I called him up to my desk and pointed to the blank line on top.

"You forgot to put your name on the paper, Thomas." I said.

He pointed to the same line on the paper and said, "No I didn't, it's right there." I bent closer to the page and looked again. There was something there, but it was so small it blended in with the line.

"I do see something, but you need to write bigger for my old eyes." I looked up, with a half smile as I tried to make it a joke.

He stood quiet for a minute and admitted in a low voice, "That's the reason I failed English class. The teachers could not read my handwriting. I can't write any bigger."

I pushed my glasses up on my nose, paused and said, "I'll have to think more about this." Thomas turned and went back to his seat.

20 Jobs: A Memoir

That afternoon I went out and bought a large magnifying glass and looked closely at Thomas's paper. Peering through the glass, the signature showed up in tiny perfect letters. This kid could write the Lord's Prayer on the head of a pin. I graded his paper using the magnifying glass and he got 100% which, after that, is what he earned on the majority of his papers that he turned in for class. Problem solved. I had no idea what Thomas would do when he got to college, but with the age of computers on our doorstep, I was sure he would figure it out.

After some minor adjustments, my senior class turned out to be as just as enjoyable as my class at Central school. We watched a PBS special about a family who volunteered to reenact homesteading during the 1800s in the West. The students were assigned to compare how different life was in present day to life a hundred years ago, a great topic for a comparison paper. We read the play *Twelve Angry Men*, which worked out well since each student had their own part. A favorite movie of the class was *The Dead Poets Society* with Robin Williams. My seniors, as I now called them, loved the idea of "carpe diem" seize the day! It always made me cry a little when the students in the movie stood on their desks to honor their teacher, Robin Williams.

Sitting at my desk, I found it impossible to believe that I had come this far from server, to celery picker, to factory worker, to secretary and now to being a real teacher. How had this happened? Then I looked down at my black, sturdy, low heeled shoes that cushioned my feet so my bunions wouldn't hurt, and thought to myself, it took you long enough.

Our last project for senior summer school was a newsletter with articles written by each student. We collaborated on who would write each article and with access to the high school library computers, we could publish the newsletter ourselves. First we brainstormed for topics and came up with a list of ideas. Brittany did a horoscope column. James wrote an article about students working while attending school. Kathy, who was finally completing her work, thanks to a call to her mother, wrote about the Summit County Fair. Thomas wrote about "Dumb Ohio Laws." It was amazing how each article fit the personality of each student and I was anxious to see the finished product.

In the last few days of class, the students were more alert and happy knowing that they were finally getting out of high school, not only for the summer, but for rest of their lives. Everyone was chatting and there was a low buzz of anticipation. Already feeling lonely knowing that these kids were moving on without me, I fiddled with the papers on my desk, head bent low.

Suddenly the room was dead quiet. I looked up to see what had happened and saw Thomas standing high on his desk top looking straight at me. My first reaction as a mother was to yell, get down before you fall, but then I realized he was offering me a tribute like the students had done for Robin Williams in *The Dead Poets Society*. A lump formed in my throat and tears welled up in my eyes. I had to do something so that the students would not see me cry, so I grabbed my camera off my desk and took a picture. On the last page of our class newsletter was a grainy black and white picture of Thomas grinning and standing high on a desk, an image that is fixed not only on paper, but forever in my memory. Carpe Diem!

Job 19 - GED Class

Remember the pleasant lady with the unstoppable, sunny smile who kept stopping by my first summer school class at Central School? Well, as it turned out that this casual meeting with Joyce provided my next job opportunity. It was fall 2005, my 7th year in the writing center at Cuyahoga Falls High School, when Joyce called unexpectedly and asked if I'd like to join the adult education staff in the Six District Compact and teach GED classes at Taylor Memorial Library in Cuyahoga Falls. She had been impressed with the positive atmosphere in my summer school classroom and remembered that the students were happy when they left my room. She thought of me when this open teaching position became available.

The teaching schedule would be two nights a week, Monday and Wednesday, from 6:00 to 8:00 in the evenings. This position would provide steady part-time employment and more money than I earned at Sylvan. Best of all, I would be working for Kent

City Schools and the earnings would be added to my teacher retirement. What a terrific opportunity!

I thanked Joyce for her offer and replied that I was extremely interested in teaching for the program, all the time thinking how random encounters can sometimes lead to fresh opportunities. Today they call it "Networking," but at that time we called it chatting in the halls. Suddenly I realized that this was the first time a job opportunity had landed in my lap, seeking me out, before I even applied for it. For a change, I didn't need my sisters, Betty or Jane, or the Help Wanted Ads. I didn't need to fill out endless applications. This position found me.

At my first GED teacher's meeting, I discovered that GED teachers taught not only reading and writing, but social studies, science and math for the state test. GED is an acronym for General Educational Development. So it covered all the subjects. English, science and social studies required careful reading and I could handle that. But math! I had never had the desire to teach that evil subject!

For an English degree, I was not required to take a math course in college and instead took one statistics class. In high school, I studied algebra and geometry for college prep, but that was a long time ago. Needless to say, they were not my best subjects.

When I graduated from Kent State, I brushed up on math in order to pass the Praxis Test that was required for a degree. I managed to pass the test by using the Praxis help book to study. Other than that, I steered clear of numbers. Well, I reasoned, if I want to succeed in this new position, I will just deal with math and learn to teach it, but my brain hurt thinking about it.

The Adult GED classes met at Taylor Memorial Library in Cuyahoga Falls. The library was in the center of the city and built around 1911. The first Monday night of GED class, I arrived at the library armed with study guides and tons of practice tests sealed in plastic all stacked in a large rolling tote bag that my daughter Amber gave me for a gift. It had been sitting in my closet since I had no need for it before, but now it became essential for hauling heavy books back and forth. My bag and I rolled into the library where I found my classroom on the lower level, a spacious meeting room located next to the periodical room and down the hall from the children's section. The room was not fancy, but it had lots of tables, chairs and a white board. I stacked my books on one of the tables, wrote my name on the white board, found my attendance sheet and waited by the door ready to greet my students when they arrived, just like Leslie had taught us to do in my education classes. "Make your students feel welcome." Leslie wisely advised.

The students filed into the room and I greeted them like long lost friends. I'd never taught adults before, but noticed that many of them were much younger than I expected. They looked a lot like my high school kids. I found out that these were students who dropped out of high school but now wanted to finish their degree, so here they were in my GED class. In fact, many of my new students were around 18 to 20 years old.

The Six District Compact would pay the cost of the GED test if students first attended our classes. If they attended classes for a couple of weeks, they could take the GED test for free. It saved them money. I later referred to them as the "in and out" crowd. Sometimes the court system assigned students to attend GED classes. Many of these students were dealing with problems in their homes and usually did not stay in our program for long. They attended some classes only because it was required and then they disappeared.

On the other side of the student spectrum were the older working adults who wanted to get their high school degree to pursue better jobs or higher education. Breaking my summer school rule, right away I decided to tell my students that I was a fairly new teacher and had earned my degree when I was older, but I didn't tell them how much older. I hoped that I looked younger than I really was. What I really wanted to convey to my adult students was the fact that you could learn new ideas or start new careers at any age.

Here I was, in my sixties, taking on a new challenge and job at an age when many people were retiring. Some friends my age had been retired for years, but I chose not to think about that. In my new GED class, I wanted to be a role model for adult students and show them that they could still learn no matter what their ages. But as it turned out, they were the role models for me.

Our adult students came to class with a variety of strengths, weaknesses and personalities. At first, I copied the Sylvan technique and used worksheets to find out what subject they needed help with, but later realized it was easier to just ask them. They answered truthfully, "I was never good at math," or "I can't even write a paragraph," or "I don't understand what I read." Being adults, they were honest and knew where they needed help. We then had a starting point.

At the beginning of each class, we did a lesson together and then students worked individually on their own lessons. Sometimes they would try a practice test, but since they became discouraged when they failed, I decided not to let anyone take the practice test until they were ready or close to ready to pass it. That worked out much better.

Fortunately for me, volunteer tutors gave freely of their time and energy to work with my students in GED classes. These tutors saved me in the math arena. Chris, a certified math-whiz teacher, was assigned as one of my tutors, and I was more than willing to let him teach most of the algebra and geometry lessons. He was a quiet man, maybe in his forties, with sandy brown hair and a thoughtful face - attentive to the students and respectful to everyone. Adult students, especially women, struggled with algebra and geometry, and truthfully, I did too.

It helped us all in class when Chris patiently stood at the white board and went over and over the process of solving fractions, decimals and square roots. He saved me a lot of headaches. By watching Chris present the lessons, I started to understand math better. When he was absent, I took over the lessons and often changed up the process of solving a problem to fit my right brain. Sometimes students said that they understood math better when I taught it, but probably they were just being kind to me.

Holly was another volunteer tutor who was very helpful. She was attractive, maybe in her 20's, with shiny blonde hair and a winning personality that put everyone at ease. She was good at tutoring English and helping with writing. Holly brightened up our classroom with her smile and sometimes with a tray of cookies or other treats. As I became better acquainted with my students and volunteers, teaching GED became less of a job; it was more like a pleasant night out with friends. It didn't hurt that I got a paycheck from the city of Kent to add to my future retirement.

I was super pleased when my niece Heather volunteered to tutor in my GED class. Heather is the daughter of my brother Joe and sister-in-law Michelle who fed me dinner when I barged in every night after my work day at Camp Asbury. Our family admired Heather because she grew from a quiet, shy country girl into an adventuresome, smart, young woman who was willing to travel and experience new cultures. She just returned from studying in Leipzig, Germany and was now attending Kent State classes. Soon she would be leaving for an internship in Washington, DC. But here and now, she wanted to volunteer as a tutor with the GED program and work with students.

Heather was also accomplished at math. She bonded with one student in particular, my oldest student, Marcy, who was probably about the same age as me, although I didn't admit that at the time. Marcy made a positive impact on our class with her eagerness to learn. But she arrived with a lot of insecurity and doubts about her ability to succeed and get a high school degree. Heather took Marcy under her wing and worked exclusively with her on math, her weakest subject. Heather took extra time to create math worksheets and even tutored Marcy outside of the classroom. They became close friends during that tutoring process.

Marcy shared that she was afraid she was not smart enough to pass the GED test and wrote about her life story in a letter. She wrote that education was not valued in her family when she was growing up and most girls were expected to find a decent man, get married and raise a family. I could identify with that era. Then Marcy told how she had a serious swimming accident that disfigured her face. Around the same time, she and her family moved to a new area where she was not accepted by other kids. They made fun of her and so she refused to go to school. Because of these circumstances, Marcy dropped out of school in eighth grade. She never remembered receiving any praise and was instead told how stupid or dumb she was. How sad to hear this story.

In spite of these early negative circumstances, Marcy always had a smile on her face. As she worked with Heather, she gained more confidence, especially with math. Our GED class took on the role as cheerleaders for Marcy and we were ecstatic when she passed her GED test on the first try. Marcy was featured in a story published in the local paper with the line above her picture - "NEVER TOO LATE FOR A DIPLOMA." We were so proud. She was the best role model for learning at any age. I smile with my heart when I think about Marcy's educational journey with Heather and how hard they both worked.

Another challenge for me in GED class was Marlene. She was in her forties with long, dark hair and high, chiseled cheek bones. She often wore exotic beaded dresses, and if I'm not mistaken, was full American Indian. Like Marcy, Marlene was a great role model for the other students. She was one of my hardest working students and faithfully attended almost all the classes. When we had conferences about our students, it worried Joyce and me because Marlene tested at a very low level in reading and math. Would we ever be able to help her pass a GED test, we wondered?

Marlene surprised us. She was a determined student and studied consistently. After numerous classes, worksheets and practice tests, she attempted the real test. Unfortunately on the first try, Marlene failed the tests, but that didn't stop her or discourage her. She kept coming to classes and continued studying. After three years and numerous attempts taking the GED tests, she passed all the parts except math, which was her weakest subject area.

During class time, Marlene would learn how to do a math problem step by step, but by the next class she would not be able to remember the steps that she did the week before. Joyce and I discussed this problem and in the end, we came to the conclusion that Marlene truly had a disability in the area of math. Unfortunately, the GED program did not recognize learning disabilities for adults. For us, that didn't matter. The tutors, her classmates and I were very proud of Marlene even if she didn't pass the math portion. We had watched her show up week after week and put in the time and hard work. She had no disability in spirit and determination. She had the "can do" spirit on her side and was an inspiration to everyone in our class.

For three years I rolled the plastic tote bag with tests and lessons through the Cuyahoga Falls Library door. Meanwhile, I continued my job in the writing Center of Cuyahoga Falls High School and applied every year for a teaching position with no luck. They would not hire me as a classroom teacher. Because of my extra pay for GED tutoring, I could now afford to take some summers off if I was careful with my money. My finances were better, but I continued to work the two jobs, writing center tutor and GED instructor.

I left the GED program on a high note. My current students all earned their GED certificates and graduated in a ceremony at Cuyahoga Falls High School, even Marlene. Joyce arranged for her to receive an "honorary" degree and the special award of the "Hardest Working" student. Needless to say, Marlene was glowing.

Holly and I lined up with the students for a final graduation picture before the ceremony. My eyes filled with tears when I saw them walk across the stage in their caps and gowns to receive their coveted diplomas. They had achieved so much! This fact showed up in their steps and the tilt of their heads held high. Looking back to those years of teaching adults, it was one of my most satisfying experiences - a ten on the job scale meter.

Still ahead of me was my 20th job - the last one before I retired. How old was I when I started this last job? Well, somewhere between 60 and 70, an age where a large percent of the population was already retired – living in Florida, lounging on white sandy beaches and taking Caribbean cruises. I, on the other hand, was about to find and begin a new challenging career, one that I never imagined.

G.H. Ashenfelter

Job 20 – Electronic Classroom of Tomorrow

Students walked the wide hallways of Cuyahoga Falls High School with their heads bent intently over their devices. Computers and cell phones were becoming the mainstream norm for most students and many adults. We still had the "no cell phone" policy in the classroom, but it was obvious that technology was challenging our school dynamics. Times were changing in Education. Many students preferred computers to books whether they were working on papers, searching for information or playing games. It was cool to be online and connected.

Online classes were trending in colleges and a variety of college classes were currently taught on the Internet. I often wondered how it might be possible to teach a class online. Personally, I already spent a great deal of time on a computer, whether in the writing center or at home, and was pretty connected for my age. So was it possible for students to learn in a remote classroom? I would soon have the chance to find the answer to that question.

It was the end of our school year, my seventh year in the writing center. Every summer I had faithfully applied for an English classroom teaching position, showed up for numerous interviews and hoped to be hired. Nonetheless, I remained an ISGI tutor. Why? I wasn't sure. I was in my sixties, so maybe my age was a hindrance, but I was totally able and willing to take on new challenges and didn't feel old. I hoped that I didn't look old, but maybe I was kidding myself.

During the last week of school, a group of teachers got together and went out for lunch to celebrate the end of the semester. We were excited about the upcoming summer as we sat at a long table in TGIFridays, menus in hand. Happy laughter mingled with talk of finishing grades and closing up classrooms for summer cleaning. Do we take posters off the walls or leave them up this year? Remember to put your name on your chair or it might disappear when they wax the floors. That happened to my chair last year. Voices buzzed and glassware clinked as I leaned in to hear the conversations further down the table. Who is retiring or leaving? When is the new baby due or who's getting married?

Suddenly my ears picked up some interesting conversation. Cindy, a fellow English teacher, was talking about another teacher, Amy, who had worked at our school as a tutor for special education – an ISGI tutor like I was. She left the Falls school system and was now teaching school online. How interesting, I thought. According to Cindy, this online job offered decent pay, benefits, teacher retirement, and best of all, teachers worked at home. Then Cindy leaned in and looked down the table straight at me and said something that changed my destiny, "This would be the perfect job for you, Gladys."

I nodded, laughed and agreed, "Yes, it would." I was after all the computer geek in our department. After lunch, I caught up with Cindy back at school and asked for Amy's phone number. She gave me her number. We said our goodbyes and walked from the building. A strange thought popped into my head - maybe this will be my last year at Cuyahoga Falls.

At home, I called Amy right away and she assured me that she loved teaching online and said that the pay was decent, and yes, they did pay into teacher retirement. That was important to me, especially at my age. I wrote down the name of the school, ECOT, which stood for Electronic Classroom of Tomorrow. ECOT was based out of Columbus and Amy told me that teachers were required to drive to Columbus, Cleveland or Cincinnati every two months for teacher meetings and parent teacher conferences. She gave me the phone number for her principal, Brett. I hung up with Amy and called him. Brett sounded friendly and affirmed that they were hiring. He told me to fill out the application online at the ECOT Website and they would get back to me. I practically ran to the computer, pulled up the application, filled it out and hit send.

Even though I applied at ECOT, I didn't put all my eggs in that online basket. I also sent in applications for English teacher positions at Cuyahoga Falls and other area schools. But in the back of my mind, I kept thinking about ECOT. I wanted to see how it would work to teach online. Could it be done effectively, I wondered? How did an online classroom function? It was a lot to think about. I settled into summer and waited to see what the future would hold.

Summer break filled up with a flurry of activities with family and friends. I was digging myself out of debt and the mortgage was getting close to being paid off in full. Finally, I was feeling more secure with my finances.

My younger son, Adam, got married in the year 2000 and was living in Fairlawn with his wife, Lori, and their daughter, Zoe. My two daughters, Earlene and Amber, were wrapped up with their lives, especially since Amber had a new little son, Nick, and Earlene had a new little daughter, Toria. It was hard to believe that I now had six grandchildren. My oldest son Earl now lived with his girlfriend out in the country in Freedom Township. I remained single in my little house in Kent.

In August, I received a call from Brett to come for an interview. He told me that ECOT would be in my area at a hotel in Beachwood, so we confirmed a time to meet. It seemed a little unusual to interview at a hotel, but considering there was no physical school, it was as good a place as any.

It was a steamy summer day when I showed up at the hotel dressed for the interview in my usual cubed black heels and a boxy, black suit with a long-sleeved jacket - my only interview suit. It would be air-conditioned, I reasoned. When I entered the hotel lobby, Brett was easy to spot. He was casually dressed in khakis and a long sleeved dark blue shirt with ECOT written across the pocket. Tall, thin and older than I expected, he probably thought the same thing about me. He fit the role of principal with his pleasant smile, easygoing manner and firm handshake. Later, I found out he was a retired principal from the Columbus Public School District.

Brett passed me off for the interview to his assistant principal, Wes, who suggested we sit by the pool since it was a beautiful day. I hesitated but then agreed. I followed him outside to the pool area and settled into a webbed deck chair. Staring at the cool blue water, I tried to ignore the blazing sun and sweat dripping down my back under the dark jacket. Besides the heat, what I remember most was that he barely asked about my qualifications and instead earnestly explained the goals of ECOT and the challenges of teaching online.

Wes seemed to be trying to convince me to accept the job as an online teacher. That surprised and confused me. He explained how the school started out small and was growing quickly. I could tell he absolutely believed in the concept of teaching online, but they were in the early stages of developing this new school. I listened and nodded in agreement. When I left the hotel, I felt confident that the job was in the bag. I wanted a challenge, right? After interviewing with Wes, it looked like being an online teacher in an up-and-coming school would fit that bill.

Soon after the interview, ECOT contacted me and required that I get fingerprinted and take a new TB test. Excited, I assumed that I was hired. I completed these requirements quickly and was ready and waiting to start my new vocation as an online teacher. A week later, I received a phone call from Brett telling me that he was sorry, but they had decided not to hire a new English teacher at this time. My hopes for a career teaching online crashed down like the newest Windows operating system. Disappointment was putting it mildly. My inner intuition had been wrong this time. I gave a heavy sigh as I gazed out the kitchen window, thankful that I had not turned in my notice at Cuyahoga Falls High School. Chin up, I consoled myself, you have your position in the writing center. Everything will be okay.

In September, I half-heartedly returned to Cuyahoga Falls. As usual, no classroom teaching position was offered. During the first weeks back in the writing center, I had a feeling of unrest like I didn't belong there anymore, but I fought it.

Then the phone call came. It was Brett. They had changed plans and now they did need an English teacher at ECOT. Did I still want the job? I screamed a silent yes! Then steadied my voice and tried not to sound over eager as I explained that I needed to break my current contract with Cuyahoga Falls and would let him know as soon as possible. I hung up and did my "got a new job" happy dance.

The very next day after the last bell rang, I ran down the wide stone steps to the school's main office, the same place where I interviewed each year for any open teacher position and was turned down flat in favor of other, supposedly better qualified, teachers. It stung to think about it. As I sat across the desk from the assistant superintendent who had denied me these opportunities, she was pleased to hear about my news and only too happy to let me out of my contract. A letter of resignation was required and that was it. Well so be it, I thought. I will teach in an English classroom even if it is an online classroom.

On the flip side of that coin, my fellow teachers seemed genuinely unhappy to see me leave, but they congratulated me on my new opportunity. I had made many friends during my seven years at the high school and I would miss them dearly. On my last day there was a staff meeting and the English teachers presented me with a large crystal heart from Tiffany and proclaimed that I was the heart of the English Department. That touched me deeply and I looked down trying to be humble, but also so they couldn't see the tears in my eyes. While I was looking down, they gave me a standing ovation, and darn, I missed it. At this moment, I was having second thoughts leaving my writing center home, but deep down knew it was time to move on even though doubts plagued me.

Would I be lonely sitting home staring at a computer screen each day? The face to face interaction with students and teachers would no longer exist. Could teaching online work out? Well, I was about to find out.

The following week, I borrowed a GPS from my niece Heather and traveled to Columbus to begin training for the online classroom at ECOT. My new laptop had arrived on my front porch and it sat beside me tucked inside its case - my new constant companion. I followed the voice directions of the GPS through a maze of Columbus streets and freeways and arrived two hours later at what looked like a shopping plaza. Approaching the entrance I saw that ECOT was printed in large, green letters on the front glass door. This was it.

I entered and found the office suite and secretary. She showed me into a plain, doctor office type lounge where I could sit and wait. A couple of other new hires were there, and being a chatty person, I bonded with a lady named Melissa who was also from the northern part of Ohio. We discussed how we had applied and ended up working at ECOT. We both wondered what we might learn that day.

As it turned out, we didn't learn much. The human resource lady demonstrated on her computer something about putting a lesson from who knows where into an unknown, invisible classroom called IQity. I watched intently but didn't understand a thing. That was the extent of the lesson. As we were leaving, I turned to Melissa and asked, "Do you know what we are doing?" She shook her head no. "Neither do I." I said. We both laughed and waved bye as we headed towards our cars to drive back north.

Thanks to the English teachers at ECOT, my confusion didn't last. During the first staff meetings in Beachwood, the other 9th grade teachers took me into their fold and walked me step by step through how to access the classroom and how to insert the English lessons into the new IQity program. I realized right away that the ECOT teachers were remarkable. They were willing to take the time to teach and share all their knowledge about teaching online. Since teachers did not work in the same building, most of our communication was accomplished on the phone or by email.

After our staff meeting, Kara, an English teacher in my department and my unofficial mentor called every Sunday night to walk me through loading the lessons into our virtual classroom for the upcoming week. She also informed me how to find and communicate with my students by posting messages in the classroom or by phoning them.

The IQity classroom was new that year at ECOT, so this was a learning curve for all the teachers. Before IQity, teachers had sent lessons back and forth by email. Now we had a program that was unfamiliar to us and the students. To make it even worse, most of that first year the IQity program was not connecting properly, or in plain language, it was down and out. We took to calling it "I-Quit-ity" for fun. As a result, we sent out lots of lessons by mail.

I repeatedly called Kara for help and advice and she never complained. She was a lovely woman in looks and spirit who patiently addressed all my concerns. Kara was a rock star in my book and her steady personality helped me through my first years. Teachers shared everything: their lessons, ideas, inspiration and computer knowledge. It's fair to say that the ECOT teachers were at that time, and probably still are today, the backbone of that online school.

The first year at ECOT passed by in a flash and here it was my second year. My summer hours had been spent figuring out how to use HTML to create my classroom pages plus writing and rewriting English lessons. Fortunately, IQity ran better thanks to the installation of new servers.

Teaching online was getting easier for me. A lot of time was spent grading, but some of our quizzes were graded automatically, thank goodness. That helped immensely since teachers generally started out with around 200 to 300 students at the beginning of each semester. To stay organized, I kept track of the students on an Excel spreadsheet. By the end of the first semester, the number of students dropped drastically. But meanwhile, hours were spent trying to get the "unresponsive" students to participate in class only to see them drop off our class list when they realized that online school was not working for them. All that time and energy was for nothing.

Some students didn't have the motivation to work independently and parents didn't back them up, so they usually dropped out within six to nine weeks and went back to attending what we called "brick and mortar" school. I quickly learned that this was the nature of online school. Studying online was not a good fit for every student, but many wanted to try. In spite of these problems, my second year went more smoothly since I was familiar with the lessons and grading. Then Elluminate came along!

Like the IQity classroom, Elluminate was a new program for teachers to master. It was a live classroom with a white board, chat options and other fun features. We could load PowerPoint Presentations onto the white board and talk to students while the lesson was displayed. This live virtual classroom added a social component for our students.

In Elluminate, students met their teachers live, heard their voices and saw them on a webcam. In addition, they chatted in real time with other students. It was the closest we could get to a traditional classroom with live interaction and discussion. Students read *To Kill a Mockingbird* out loud in parts, played Jeopardy, or reviewed quiz questions. I demonstrated how to write five paragraph essays on the white board and shared model essays, such fun stuff for English teachers. I enjoyed teaching in

Elluminate class and took to it like a kid with a new bike, or nowadays a kid with a new Xbox.

Students were highly encouraged to attend Elluminate classes, but unfortunately, it was not required because ECOT advertised the school as having a flexible schedule. If a student didn't want to attend a live class, they didn't have to. Because of this, I bribed students with extra credit and the promise of "great fun" if they attended.

Elluminate classes were recorded and linked in the IQity classroom. I advertised my Elluminate schedule on my home page and in posts and told little white lies stating that students who came to our live classroom had better grades. It worked a little because a higher number of students attended my Elluminate classes. I was puffed up about that until I found out that higher Elluminate attendance didn't help my overall passing rate, which was about the same as other classrooms. The students who already worked hard and were on target to pass were the ones who attended Elluminate. Most students ignored my pleas to attend the live classes. That was disappointing.

In an online school, the passing rate was dismal at best. ECOT staff and the teachers always tried to remedy that problem. Keep in mind that our population of students was the ones who were most likely failing in their former schools. They came to us with problems. But I do believe the school was seriously searching for the best and most effective ways to teach classes online. Our English department constantly analyzed what lessons and techniques worked best for our students. Our school was an experiment and this experiment in education was growing faster than anyone predicted, year by year. We had to grow with it.

ECOT was founded in the year 2000 by a man named Bill Lager. In 2001, 21 kids graduated from the new online school. This number would increase faster than anyone expected. Bill Lager had a vision and a passion to bring education to every student no matter what the circumstances in their lives, be it poverty, crime filled districts or illness. You can read more about his vision for online education in his book *The Kids That ECOT Taught*.

In his book, Mr. Lager wrote about the many different reasons that each student had for enrolling in ECOT. Some students needed more flexibility either to work a job or work at their own pace. Some were looking for a safe learning environment in our sometimes dangerous world. Whatever the reasons, I believe that Bill Lager had it right. Students needed a choice. Truly he had the interests of the students in mind when he started his innovative online school.

When I told people that I taught at ECOT, an online school, they exclaimed, "Oh, wow! That sounds terrific to work at home and teach on the computer." I nodded and flashed my cool online teacher smile. Then their first question was generally, "What types of students want to attend school online?" Then I had to pause and think because this question was not easy to answer.

The longer I taught at ECOT the better I understood our students and their reasons for enrolling in our school. At the end of each semester, I asked students to write what they liked or didn't like about being an online student. After reading these answers and talking to students and their parents, I formed a clearer picture of why they chose ECOT. Their stories coincided a lot with Bill Lager's reasons for pioneering his school. Over and over, one of the biggest reasons students chose ECOT was because they were bullied and there was too much drama at their school.

Bullying has made headlines on the news lately and my students confirmed that it is alive and well in a majority of schools. Many of our students lived well below poverty level and attended schools in larger districts like Columbus, Cincinnati, Akron, or Cleveland. At these schools there were often dangerous gang problems to go along with the bullying. Students felt threatened. Working online offered a safer environment for students who lived in large inner-city school districts.

Health issues were another main reason some students came to ECOT. If a young person had diabetes or any other serious health problems, they often missed a lot of school and failed because of their attendance records. Learning at home on a computer, diabetic students could eat whenever necessary or attend doctor appointments without being considered truant. They simply completed their work later in the day. Students and parents were relieved from the constant worry of juggling school with illness and doctor visits.

One of my students, a 9th grader, lived with the horror of his father's illness caused by a brain tumor. He was close with his dad and didn't want to leave him to go to school. It turned out that he was an excellent ECOT student and had no issues completing his school work from his home. Another example was a young lady who took care of her grandmother who was partially disabled and in a wheelchair. This student worked hard, attended Elluminate classes and kept up with her lessons while she assisted her grandmother at their home. These stories tugged at my heart strings. I was becoming more aware of the importance of online school. It was an alternative way for students to get an education when circumstances were stacked against them.

Along with illness and bullying, a number of girls enrolled at ECOT because they were pregnant or just had a baby. My inbox was often full of new baby pictures. Their happy faces made me smile and I always commented back on how cute their babies looked. Then I shook my head sadly as I realized that teen pregnancy was reaching epidemic proportions in our society and these young moms or dads would be faced with a more difficult future. Fortunately our school offered these teens a chance to keep up with their studies and earn a diploma in between night feedings and changing diapers. ECOT allowed students in any situation to complete their high school courses online and so many teens and parents were grateful for this opportunity.

Economic conditions were another legitimate reason for finishing high school online. Students and their families were sometimes faced with economic hardships due to lack of employment, high cost of living or maybe a divorce in their family. Many older teens worked full time jobs while attending our school. They needed flexible schedules and ECOT provided that schedule. I realized that Bill Lager had it right when he founded ECOT. It really did fill a need for many students.

On the flip side, some students listed less important reasons for enrolling in ECOT saying "I couldn't get up in the morning." Or, "My teachers wouldn't help me." Or, "The bus doesn't come by my house and I don't drive." If students were unmotivated to keep up with their work online, they eventually were forced to withdraw and go back to brick and mortar schools. By asking this question of students about why they chose ECOT, I saw a better picture of issues that students face today. An online school was a good fit for many different situations but not for every situation. Bill Lager's vision of learning online helped many students graduate when they might have become another statistical drop out. Our school kept growing.

I established a routine for working at home. My typical work day began at 8:00 a.m. when I got dressed and went to my subterranean classroom, otherwise known as my basement. I refused to work in my pajamas like some teachers and couldn't take myself seriously until I was dressed, but still in comfortable clothes, stretchy, soft and warm - no shoes, just slippers. My makeshift office room was next door to the washer and dryer, but fortunately far away from the refrigerator. Often I took a cup of coffee or tea downstairs, but no food. I ate meals upstairs away from my work space.

A long, printed sheet hung from the doorway and separated my office from the laundry room, very classy. I pushed aside the sheet, entered and turned on my little heater to warm up the room. Then I opened up my black Toshiba laptop, hit the start button and waited for it to boot up.

A lined tablet and calendar sat next to my computer with names, notes and activities written for each day. Which students did I call yesterday? Which ones did I need to call again? Any meetings for the day were marked on the calendar. This kept my priorities straight. With hundreds of students, I needed all the help I could get.

After the computer booted up, I checked my email and answered messages. Next I went into the virtual classroom and answered posts from students. Many students didn't understand that the little "inbox" symbol at the top right in the blue sky of the classroom was a message center, so there were usually not many messages. From there, I clicked on my Home Page and made sure the information was current. Then I checked the assignment pages to see how many lessons were completed by my students.

A PowerPoint presentation must be ready for the live class in Elluminate and sometimes that took an hour or more. I preferred to make my own PowerPoint lessons and enjoyed creating the pages adding pictures and designs. These were saved and shared with other teachers. At noon I went upstairs for a half hour lunch and went back down to log in exactly at 12:30. My Elluminate classes were from 1:00 to 1:45 and office hours lasted till 3:00. I often worked later, including many evenings and weekends to keep up with grading and planning. Working online, days passed like a flicker on the screen and so did the weeks and months. It was never boring.

Every couple of months, teachers traveled to meetings in Columbus. I often rode down with teacher friends from my area, including Amy who first told me about working online. At the meetings, English teachers shared new techniques and creative lessons to use in our classrooms. Twice a year, part of our conference time was used for parent teacher conferences and it was very uplifting to finally meet some of my students and their parents.

After two days of meetings, I felt refreshed and eager to try out the new ideas that were shared. But during the time away, teachers' classrooms went unattended. No substitutes at ECOT unless you took a long term leave. After meetings, I was behind on my work, so even though I was keen to try out the inspiring techniques and helpful ideas, I was faced with playing classroom time catch-up. Still, my skills improved each year.

G.H. Ashenfelter

Numbers for graduation grew larger every year when I taught at ECOT. In 2001, 21 students graduated from ECOT. In my last year of teaching, 2013, 2,500 students graduated from ECOT at the Schottenstein Center in Columbus. Our guest speaker was Jack Hannah from the Columbus Zoo. The year before, our graduation speaker was John Kasich, the governor of Ohio. Our graduations were gala events.

I volunteered as a line leader for graduations at Cuyahoga Falls High School and also for graduations at ECOT. At the Cuyahoga Falls graduation, which was held at Blossom Music Center, I led the students across the stage to receive their diplomas. The seniors were excited and proud and their happy faces beamed from below the symbolic, square hats that represented an important step in life. Gowns floated and billowed out over heels, dress shoes, flip-flops. The senior class at Cuyahoga Falls numbered around 400 students and the ceremony lasted a couple of hours. Taking part in the graduation was one of my fondest memories from Falls High School.

In comparison, imagine the length of the ceremony at ECOT with 2,500 students. Although every student did not attend, it was a grand marathon graduation that needed to be held on a Saturday or Sunday. The students' faces were still beaming, but the day stretched long for the parents, teachers and staff. Unless there was a good excuse, ECOT teachers were pretty much required to help in some capacity during the graduation ceremony at the Schottenstein Center. Being a volunteer line leader, I arrived early to greet students and help them find their seats on the main floor of the huge auditorium. We sat at the end of each row and led students up to the stage to accept their diplomas.

By the time the ceremony began, I had been up for hours and driven the two hour trip to Columbus. The graduation lasted about six hours from start to finish. It was a twelve hour day, but so worth it to see the looks on the students' faces when they received their diplomas. A huge screen in front flashed the smiles of each student for families to see. Even though ECOT was an online school, different from the Falls, the students' faces beamed with the same smiles of accomplishment. We did it! We graduated! What a thrill to be a part of this special moment for my students at Cuyahoga Falls and at ECOT.

In my last years of teaching at ECOT, the office came up with a new directive. Teachers were required to contact each student on their roster at least once during a nine week period and complete a short lesson with them. This sounds reasonable, but remember we started out with around 200 to 300 students each semester. Then that number dwindled down to about 150 by the end of the nine week grading period. Therefore, many hours were spent on phone calls during the first weeks of school trying to reach a large number of students who eventually dropped out.

G.H. Ashenfelter

Each day, I called students who had two to three contact numbers, and left messages for them to call me back. Most of the time they didn't! It surprised me to find out how difficult it was to reach a parent or student especially when they had home phones and cell phones. Sometimes students called me back, but mainly I had to contact them. A big part of my day was now spent on the telephone. We used Cisco office phones that were directly linked to the main office. Teachers knew that ECOT kept track of how many calls we made and the duration. We knew because each week the office sent us an email with a listing of calls and how many minutes we spent on each call. No pressure! And, no pretending to call, you had to call.

This extended phone time along with Elluminate class didn't leave much time during the day to prepare and grade lessons. It was especially difficult for English teachers who had to grade numerous writing assignments. I know, many English teachers say that, but it was true. It takes a lot of time to grade and comment on essays or research papers. Many times I felt overwhelmed with grading papers along with phoning students.

With the added phone calls, work spilled over even more into evenings and weekends. I worked practically every Sunday in order to load the next week's lessons into the classroom and catch up on any past grading. Even though other teachers took the phone calls in stride, eventually I became weary of being on the phone so much. I believe this new policy was one of the main reasons that I started to feel dissatisfied with my online teaching job. I felt like a combination truant officer and telemarketer. I was continually trying to reach students and encourage them to get online and finish their work. I knew it was important to make connections with students, but I started thinking that this was not really teaching.

The laptop was once my loveable constant companion, but after seven years my computer work haunted my dreams with images of little boxes shuffling around on a screen inside my head. I often woke up tired. My brain didn't shut down as I continued to work in my sleep. During the summers, I didn't want to open or even look at my laptop. It had lost its former luster.

ECOT paid a decent wage, over $30,000 a year with steady raises and bonuses. Since I made more money, much more than I made as a tutor at Cuyahoga Falls, I no longer had to work a summer job, so at the close of each summer of freedom from the classroom, getting back online in the fall was becoming harder and harder.

When I started back one fall semester and turned on the webcam at the live Elluminate classes, some students said I looked like their grandmother. Well, no wonder! The camera did not lie about my age. That is when I knew retirement was imminent. I wanted more time for my family and extra time to pursue new interests. Even though I often said that working at ECOT from home was like being retired with a job, I no longer felt that was the case. I longed for more free time to spend with family and friends. In 2013, I turned 70 and decided it was time to retire.

∞∞∞∞∞∞∞∞∞∞

When I started my first job as a carhop at age 14, I couldn't visualize where my journey would take me. It was one day at a time for me. I held no thoughts for my future back then. But the years passed all too quickly.

My life was filled with good times: birthdays, graduations, new babies, weddings, and special gatherings with family and friends. These milestones and celebrations, while so important, were not all included in this memoir; however, they are forever held dear in my heart.

There were also bad times in my life. Mistakes I regret. Time spent being my own worst enemy, choosing wrong roads and unsuitable lovers - along with making bad decisions. Many of these events were not included in this memoir. Instead, I chose to write around those experiences, good or bad, to remain true to the theme of writing about my twenty jobs.

My twenty jobs were not spectacular. They were jobs that anyone could do. I didn't save the world or invent new products. I'm not special in any way and no monuments will be raised in my honor. After writing this memoir, I've decided it's not just the special people who hold this world together. It is the average Joes and Janes who show up every day on the job to serve people, or make a product, or pick the crop, or file the papers, or clean the spaces, or take care of the children and elderly. It is the workers who drive the trucks or buses, stock the shelves, build the houses and teach the children. The common people make up our real world and shape it into what it is today and will be tomorrow. There should be no apologizing for hard work.

Having lived through my working life, once in real time and again in my memory, I believe these job experiences shaped me into the person I am today; someone who is not afraid to try new things and not afraid to face the inevitable changes in life. Looking back, I wouldn't change a thing even if I could.

Readers were warned at the beginning that I was not lucky in love, so I didn't end up marrying Prince Charming or finding my true soul mate. Sorry to say, that just didn't happen. Or am I really sorry? Honestly, I am content with my life and cherish every single minute of time spent with family and friends and appreciate the freedom to schedule my day without the constraints of a job schedule. I had that pressure for many years.

∞∞∞∞∞∞∞∞

What do retired people do after working for years? Well, I added some new activities. I joined a gym and took swim aerobic classes; I took up quilting and met with friends in southern Ohio at least once a month to cut up material and sew it back together again. I attended quilt retreats and quilt shows with my best friend Barbie and scheduled in some bus trips. Barbie and I flew to Florida to visit Jan and we all three sailed away together on an Alaskan cruise. Lovely! This is what retired people do. They savor life.

Providentially, I joined a Family Folklore story writing group at the Stow Library. The members encouraged me to write more and to finally finish this memoir. Our group met each week and sat around a large conference table to read our stories out loud. When I read my chapters, they leaned forward and listened carefully to every word. I could not have paid for a better audience and may never have finished this memoir without their support. They asked helpful questions and encouraged me to keep writing.

Because of the Family Folklore writing group, I became interested in genealogy and began writing family stories and working on my family tree. I joined the online "Find-a-Grave" community where you look for cemetery graves and take pictures of tombstones to add information about family members. My family collectively groaned when they found out that I happily roamed around cemeteries to photograph deceased relatives' graves. Just in case that wasn't enough to keep me busy, I joined a monthly book club at the Kent Free Library and continued to pursue one of my favorite pastimes, reading. No doubt, retirement is proving to be an active time in my life. I feel blessed!

Most of my family lives close by so I can spend time with my grandchildren. Hard to believe, but I have six grandchildren: April, Melissa, Michael, Toria, Nick and Zoe; and five great grandsons: Tyler, Elijah, Evan, Ethan, and Jordan. They bring me joy.

My two sisters, Betty and Jane, and my brother Joe are still in my life. We often talk by phone and sometimes visit. Betty is retired and she and her husband Jim now live in Florida most of the year. Jane and her husband Ray live about half an hour away. My brother Joe and his wife Michelle still live close enough that I still stop in for free dinners once in awhile. They like to play Euchre and I still like to read lots of books. We are different in many ways but joined together by our shared memories.

∞∞∞∞∞∞∞∞

Written memories are not always exact, so keep in mind that a memoir consists of selected details as they are remembered. It is not a biography based on proven facts. This is a memoir based on my recollections. I hope when my children and grandchildren read this book, they are inspired to try their hand at new ventures and if it doesn't work out for the best, change directions, move on and try something else. They will keep learning and growing throughout their lives. They will live their own lives and create their own stories, but I hope that my words will inspire them in some small way.

G.H. Ashenfelter

In writing this, I realize that I take after my dad. We are both practical and believe in hard-work. Because of him, I chose to write about my jobs. Now that my past has been viewed through the distance of time and memory, I find it acceptable. For now I am content to be retired, at least until my next job, maybe as a writer.

83017648R00159

Made in the USA
Columbia, SC
22 December 2017